Letts
gets you through

In partnership with

11+ TUTORING

GET TEST-READY

PRACTICE TEST PAPERS

Get test-ready
Book 2

11+
FOR CEM

4 test papers

- Comprehension
- Verbal Reasoning
- Maths
- Non-Verbal Reasoning

PRACTICE TEST PAPERS

11+

PHILIP McMAHON

Contents

Guidance notes for parents

What your child will need to sit these papers

- A quiet place to sit the exam
- A clock which is visible to your child
- A way to play the audio download
- A pencil and an eraser
- A piece of paper

Your child should not use a calculator for any of these papers.

How to invigilate the test papers

Your child should sit Test C, Paper 1 then have a 15-minute break. They should then sit Paper 2. Don't help your child or allow any talking. Review the answers with your child and help improve their weaker areas. At a later date, your child should sit Test D, Papers 1 and 2 in a two-hour session.

Step 1: Remove the answers and keep them hidden from your child.

Step 2: Remove the answer sheet section. Your child should write their full name on top of the first answer sheet. Give them the question paper booklet. They must not open the paper until they are told to do so by the audio instructions.

Step 3: Start the audio.

Step 4: Ask your child to work through the practice questions before the time starts for each section. An example is already marked on each section of the answer sheet. Your child should mark the answer sheet clearly and check that the practice questions are correctly marked.

Step 5: Mark the answer sheet. Then, together with your child, work through the questions that were answered incorrectly. When working through the Non-verbal Reasoning sections, ensure you have the question papers open to help explain the answers to your child.

How your child should complete the answer sheet

Your child MUST NOT write their answers on the question paper, they must use the answer sheet. They should put a horizontal line through the boxes on the answer sheet. To change an answer, your child should fully erase the incorrect answer and then clearly select a new answer. Any rough workings should be done on a separate piece of paper.

The audio instructions

Both papers have audio instructions to allow your child to learn, listen and act upon audio instructions. Audio instructions are at the start, during and at the end of the sections. Audio warnings on the time remaining will be given at varying intervals. Your child should listen out for these warnings.

The symbols at the foot of the page

Written instructions are at the foot of the page. Your child MUST follow these instructions:

Continue working

Stop and wait for instructions

Your child can review questions within the allocated time, but must not move onto the next section until they are allowed to do so.

The instructions and examples at the beginning of the section

In the instructions, your child should look for: the time allowed; how many questions there are; and how to complete the answers.

Examples are at the beginning of every section to show the type of question included in a particular section. The example questions will be worked through as part of the audio instructions.

Developing time-management skills and working at speed

These test papers have been used with previous pupils of the CEM exam in various counties. They provide essential practice of the types of questions which could arise, in addition to the strictly timed conditions, which will help your child practise their time-management skills.

Marking the papers

Each question is worth one mark.

Scores

Overall scores your child should be aiming for:

• 75% or more on the first pack of 2 papers if taken in the weeks leading up to the exam

• 70% or more on the second pack of 2 papers if taken in the weeks leading up to the exam.

A weighted score attaches a certain amount of weight to each section in the exam.

How to work out your child's score:

Add together the scores for Non-verbal Reasoning and Maths sections (both Numeracy and Problem Solving). This will give you score A. This relates to both sections in all papers.

Then add together the remaining scores for all English sections, which will give you score B.

Then add scores A and B together and divide them by 2.

This will give you an average weighted score across the 2 packs.

To calculate your child's weighted score as a percentage, divide your child's score by the maximum score, and multiply it by 100.

Once you have completed this, you will have two percentages and the combined weighted score across the two papers is the middle of these two percentages.

For example: If your child scores 46 out of 92 for English, this equals 50%.

If your child scores 62 out of 82, this equals approximately 76%. So the combined weighted score across the two papers is 50% + 76%, which equals 126%. If you divide this by 2, this equals 63%. This is your child's weighted score.

The maximum scores:

Test C Paper 1 English – 39

Test C Paper 1 Maths and Non-verbal Reasoning – 48

Test C Paper 2 English – 57

Test C Paper 2 Maths and Non-verbal Reasoning – 25

Test D Paper 1 English – 30

Test D Paper 1 Maths and Non-verbal Reasoning – 43

Test D Paper 2 English – 57

Test D Paper 2 Maths and Non-verbal Reasoning – 25

English maximum scores, Test C Papers 1 and 2 – 96

Maths and Non-verbal Reasoning maximum scores, Test C Papers 1 and 2 – 73

English maximum scores, Test D Papers 1 and 2 – 87

Maths and Non-verbal Reasoning maximum scores, Test D Papers 1 and 2 – 68

Please note the following:

As the content varies from year to year in CEM exams, a good score in this paper does not guarantee a pass, and a lower score may not always suggest a fail!

What happens if your child does not score a good mark?

Identify strengths and weaknesses

Continue to provide a wide variety of questions to build your child's knowledge. Focus on the areas in which your child did not perform as well.

Timings

Allow your child to continue practising working under timed conditions.

Test C Paper 1

Instructions

1. Ensure you have pencils and an eraser with you.
2. Make sure you are able to see a clock or watch.
3. Write your name on the answer sheet.
4. Do not open the question booklet until you are told to do so by the audio instructions.
5. Listen carefully to the audio instructions given.
6. Mark your answers on the answer sheet only.
7. All workings must be completed on a separate piece of paper.
8. You should not use a calculator, dictionary or thesaurus at any point in this paper.
9. Move through the papers as quickly as possible and with care.
10. Follow the instructions at the foot of each page.
11. You should mark your answers with a horizontal strike, as shown on the answer sheet.
12. If you want to change your answer, ensure that you rub out your first answer and that your second answer is clearly more visible.
13. You can go back and review any questions that are within the section you are working on only. You must await further instructions before moving onto another section.

Symbols and Phrases used in the Tests

 Instructions
 Time allowed for this section
 Stop and wait for further instructions
 Continue working

Comprehension

INSTRUCTIONS

YOU HAVE 8 MINUTES TO COMPLETE THE FOLLOWING SECTION.

YOU HAVE 10 QUESTIONS TO COMPLETE WITHIN THE TIME GIVEN.

EXAMPLES

Comprehension Example

Some people choose to start their Christmas shopping early in October. It has been reported that some people even buy their Christmas presents in the sales in August. In recent years, people have the option of purchasing their Christmas presents online.

Example 1

According to the passage, what is the earliest that people start their Christmas shopping?

A   In the preceding summer
B   In the preceding October
C   In the preceding November
D   Christmas Eve
E   In early December

The correct answer is A. This has already been marked in Example 1 in the Comprehension section of your answer sheet.

Practice Question 1

What has caused a change in how people shop, in recent years?

A   There are more shops.
B   Shops are more crowded.
C   You can easily organise your journey to the shops.
D   New products are available
E   There has been a rise in use of the Internet

The correct answer is E. Please mark this in Practice Question 1 in the Comprehension section of your answer sheet.

STOP AND WAIT FOR FURTHER INSTRUCTIONS

The Popularity of Allotments

The changing of the seasons can be clearly seen in allotments, which are often located on the periphery of residential areas in Britain. Allotments are pieces of land divided into plots and then allocated to families or individuals. Allotments, which were once left barren, have once again

Line 5   become popular with young people wanting to be self-sufficient, providing the majority of their food for themselves and their young families. They do however, require a significant investment of time and energy.

The winter months are often a period of inactivity. The ground is too hard for much work to happen, and the weather too cold for many crops to grow.

Line 10   Once spring has sprung, the allotments become a hive of activity with everyone attending their plots at least once a fortnight. At this stage in the year, the work is ploughing and sowing the vegetables, which the allotment holders hope will grow in abundance from that point onwards. In a good year, when the conditions are right, there should be a plentiful harvest.

Line 15   With the onset of summer, the work changes. Regular watering is needed to ensure that the crops do not wilt and die. There is often an additional peril in the form of insects, which can engulf and devastate the crops. The treatment of these pests depends on the allotment holders' beliefs, as to whether they want to use pesticides or natural, environmentally-friendly

Line 20   alternatives, to defeat an infestation. Traditional methods, such as nets placed over brassicas (purple sprouting broccoli) can ward off butterflies from laying their eggs. If one butterfly lays its eggs here, an entire crop can be destroyed as a result. When the sun is shining the weeds also grow and this means that hoeing is required on a weekly basis.

Line 25   In the autumn months, most of the crops are harvested and enjoyed. Many are cut down in preparation for the following year. Expertise and knowledge of the individual varieties of all the crops are required. An amateur allotment holder needs to learn about sowing, growing and harvesting to ensure a plentiful yield.

Line 30   The waiting lists for allotments are growing year by year as their popularity increases. Allotments are normally held for a generation, resulting in long waiting lists of many years in some places.

1   Read the passage above and answer the following questions.

In the context of the passage, what type of word is the word 'allocated'?

- **A**   Metaphor
- **B**   Noun
- **C**   Verb
- **D**   Homophone
- **E**   Adjective

CONTINUE WORKING ⏵

(2) According to the passage, which phrase best describes the current situation with allotments?

A Allotments are very popular
B Nobody wants an allotment
C Allotments are very expensive to buy
D Allotments are mainly held by older people
E Allotments are reversing

(3) According to the passage, which of the following best describes the following phrase:

'a significant investment of time and energy'?

A Allotments need power
B Allotments are very expensive
C Allotments need expertise
D Allotments can be bought and sold
E Allotments require people to spend time and effort

(4) According to the passage, which phrase best describes what happens in the winter months?

A People attend every two weeks
B People attend every week
C Crops grow well in the winter
D Nothing happens
E Allotment holders harvest their crops

(5) In the context of the passage, what is the meaning of 'a hive of activity'?

A A place where bees live
B A busy place
C A place which is extremely quiet
D A place where people go to be active
E A place to have some time alone

(6) What is the meaning of 'abundance'?

A A large quantity
B A small quantity
C A straight line
D A regular pattern
E A haphazard way

CONTINUE WORKING ⇨

7 Which word is the most similar to 'engulf'?

    A   Formulate
    B   Harden
    C   Arrange
    D   Envelop
    E   Be aware of

8 According to the passage, how often should 'hoeing' be completed?

    A   Every three weeks
    B   Every ten days
    C   Once a fortnight
    D   Every five days
    E   Every seven days

9 Which word is the most similar to the phrase 'ward off'?

    A   Worshipful
    B   General
    C   Aggregate
    D   Repel
    E   Trustworthy

10 According to the passage, describe the grammatical term for 'yield' within the context of the sentence, 'a plentiful yield'.

    A   Verb
    B   Noun
    C   Adjective
    D   Metaphor
    E   Simile

STOP AND WAIT FOR FURTHER INSTRUCTIONS

Grammar

INSTRUCTIONS

 YOU HAVE 5 MINUTES TO COMPLETE THE FOLLOWING SECTION.

YOU HAVE 9 QUESTIONS TO COMPLETE WITHIN THE TIME GIVEN.

EXAMPLES

Read the passage below and answer the 9 questions that follow. There are some mistakes in the use of capital letters and punctuation. In some questions there may be no errors.

> The dogs were running in the garden. As the postman opened the gate, the dogs started biting the postman's leg.

Example 1

Look at the following options taken from the above passage. Select the option that contains a punctuation or grammar error, if any.

A	B	C	D	E
The dogs	were	in the	garden	No errors

The correct answer is E. This has already been marked in Example 1 in the Grammar section of your answer sheet.

Practice Question 1

Look at the following options taken from the above passage. Select the option that contains a punctuation or grammar error, if any.

A	B	C	D	E
As the postman	the dogs	biting	the postmans	No errors

The correct answer is D. Please mark the answer D in Practice Question 1 in the Grammar section of your answer sheet.

STOP AND WAIT FOR FURTHER INSTRUCTIONS

Read the passage below and answer the 9 questions that follow. There are some mistakes in the use of capital letters and punctuation. In some questions there may be no errors.

Emily and Laura were sisters. Laura was the elder of the two sisters. They were heading out to drop of some clothes at the local jumble sale. Laura carried a large bag of clothes to the village hall jumble sale. she could not see in front of herself and tripped on the uneven pavement. She nearly got a bad accident. Luckily Emily caught her as she fell. After dropping off the bag of clothes, they had a quick browse at what was on offer.

"This jacket of mine is wore out," remarked Emily. "I'll see if I can get a new one here."

Whilst perusing the clothes, Laura realised she hurted her leg when she nearly fell over earlier. They decided to head home after emily realised there were no suitable jackets to buy. "Lets run home together," said Emily, but after a while Laura said, "I cannot run no further."

Look at the following sentences from the above passage and select the answer from below that has a grammatical or punctuation error, if any.

1. Laura was the elder of the two sisters.

A	B	C	D	E
Laura	was	elder	sisters	No errors

2. she could not see in front of herself and tripped on the uneven pavement.

A	B	C	D	E
in front	could not	she	pavement.	No errors

3. She nearly got a bad accident.

A	B	C	D	E
She	nearly	got	a bad	No errors

4. "This jacket of mine is wore out," remarked Emily.

A	B	C	D	E
"This	jacket of	out," remarked	is wore out,"	No errors

CONTINUE WORKING

(5) "I'll see if I can get a new one here."

A	B	C	D	E
"I'll	see if	I can get	a new one here."	No errors

(6) Whilst perusing the clothes, Laura realised she hurted her leg when she nearly fell over earlier.

A	B	C	D	E
Whilst perusing	the clothes,	she hurted her leg	when she nearly	No errors

(7) They decided to head home after emily realised there were no suitable jackets to buy.

A	B	C	D	E
They decided to	head home after	emily realised	jackets to buy	No errors

(8) "Lets run home together," said Emily, but after a while Laura said, "I cannot run no further."

A	B	C	D	E
"Lets run	home together,"	said Emily,	but after	No errors

(9) "Lets run home together," said Emily, but after a while Laura said, "I cannot run no further."

A	B	C	D	E
said Emily,	while Laura said,	"I cannot run	no further	No errors

STOP AND WAIT FOR FURTHER INSTRUCTIONS ⊗

Numeracy

 YOU HAVE 19 MINUTES TO COMPLETE THE FOLLOWING SECTION.

YOU HAVE 39 QUESTIONS TO COMPLETE WITHIN THE TIME GIVEN.

EXAMPLES

Example 1

Calculate 53 – 42

A   12   **B**   1   **C**   4   **D**   5   **E**   11

The correct answer is E. This has already been marked in Example 1 in the Numeracy section of your answer sheet.

Practice Question 1

Calculate 95 – 75

A   21   **B**   20   **C**   19   **D**   18   **E**   13

The correct answer is B. Please mark this in Practice Question 1 in the Numeracy section of your answer sheet.

STOP AND WAIT FOR FURTHER INSTRUCTIONS

1 What is the number if 21 is three times more than half of this number?

A 36 **B** 48 **C** 126 **D** 7 **E** 14

2 Select the appropriate number or numbers to complete the sequence in place of the ? in the sequence below.

31, 32, 34, ?, 41

A 35 **B** 36 **C** 37 **D** 38 **E** 39

3 Select the appropriate numbers to complete the subtraction in place of the ? in the incomplete calculation below.

Your choice of answers is written as the missing numbers should appear in the question from left to right.

```
  ? 9 ? 4
- 7 8 ?
---------
  4 ? 3 3
```

A 4, 1, 1, 1 **B** 4, 1, 2, 1 **C** 3, 9, 8, 7
D 3, 1, 1, 1 **E** 4, 1, 2, 2

4 My journey by car across London in the rush hour averages 8 mph. The distance of the journey is 1.6 miles. How long does the journey take?

A 4 minutes **B** 5 minutes **C** 16 minutes
D 15 minutes **E** 12 minutes

5 Susan works in a café and gets a staff discount of 20% on all food and drink that she purchases there. She has lunch in the café every weekday. She spends £24 each week in the café on her lunch. What is the value of the discount on her food purchased in the café each week?

A £8 **B** £4 **C** £5 **D** £6 **E** £4.80

6 Mohammed is 4 years older than Emily's brother, William. Emily and William are twins. If Emily is 7, how old is Mohammed?

A 3 **B** 11 **C** 9 **D** 12 **E** 4

CONTINUE WORKING

7 Arrange the following in order of size, from smallest to largest.

101 mm, 10.11 cm, $\frac{1}{10}$ m, 10 km, 11 cm

A $\frac{1}{10}$ m, 101 mm, 10.11 cm, 11 cm, 10 km

B   101 mm, $\frac{1}{10}$ m, 10.11 cm, 11 cm, 10 km

C $\frac{1}{10}$ m, 10.11 cm, 101 mm, 11 cm, 10 km

D $\frac{1}{10}$ m, 101 mm, 11 cm, 10.11 cm, 10 km

E $\frac{1}{10}$ m, 10km, 101 mm, 10.11 cm, 11 cm

8 Select the only equation that is incorrect.

A   453 − 2 = 452 − 0
B   5,868 − 1,869 = 3,999
C   901 = 1001 − 10 × 10
D   65 = 3 × 21 + 2
E   86 = 50 + 2 × 18

9 Calculate 26^2.

A   767   B   520   C   176   D   576   E   676

10 Identify the number that the vertical arrow is pointing to on the number line.

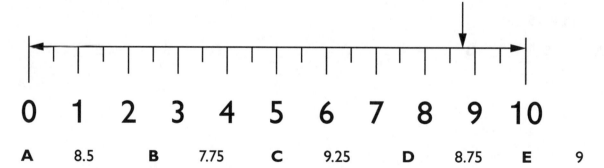

A   8.5   B   7.75   C   9.25   D   8.75   E   9

11 Calculate 3 hours and 55 minutes on from 9:25 a.m.

A   12:20 p.m.   B   1:20 p.m.   C   1 p.m.
D   10:25 a.m.   E   11:25 a.m.

CONTINUE WORKING ▶

(12) Calculate $\frac{1}{3} \div 3$

A $\frac{3}{9}$ B 2   C $\frac{1}{9}$ D $\frac{1}{8}$ E $\frac{4}{6}$

(13) Which number is half way between 23 and 7?

A 15   B 16   C 25   D 15.5   E 14.5

(14) A map has a scale of 1 : 500,000. If two churches are 5 mm apart on the map, how far apart are they in real life?

A 10,000 m   B 6,500 m   C 125 km
D 100 km   E 2,500 m

(15) How many grams are there in 0.52 kg?

A 250   B 52   C 5,200
D 520   E 7

(16) Calculate 1.1% of 70.

A 0.77   B 0.66   C 0.55   D 0.5   E 0.4

(17) Select the number to go in place of the question mark.

? × 15 = 75

A 5   B 4   C 3   D 6   E 7

CONTINUE WORKING ⇨

18 Look at the chart below and answer the question that follows.

The chart shows the favourite hobby of each child in a class.

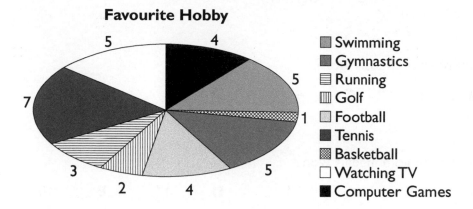

Favourite Hobby

Legend:
- Swimming
- Gymnastics
- Running
- Golf
- Football
- Tennis
- Basketball
- Watching TV
- Computer Games

Which is the least favourite hobby of the children in the class?

A   Tennis   **B**   Gymnastics   **C**   Watching TV
D   Basketball   **E**   Swimming

Look at the chart below and answer the questions that follow.

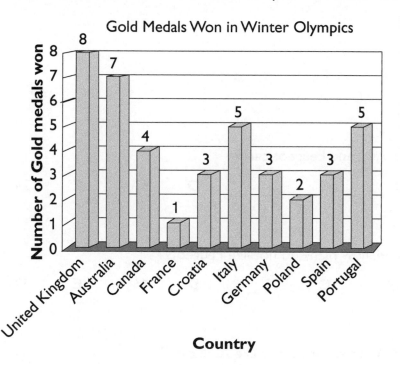

Gold Medals Won in Winter Olympics

19 What is the mode number of gold medals won?

A   3   **B**   4   **C**   5   **D**   6   **E**   7

CONTINUE WORKING

20 Which country won the second most gold medals?

| A | United Kingdom | B | Australia | C | Portugal |
| D | Spain | E | Germany | | |

21 What is the median number of medals won?

A 3.5   **B** 3   **C** 4   **D** 5   **E** 6

22 What is the mean number of gold medals won?

A 4   **B** 4.5   **C** 3.1   **D** 4.1   **E** 10

Look at the Venn diagram below, which shows the number of children that like certain types of cars, then answer the questions that follow.

Children

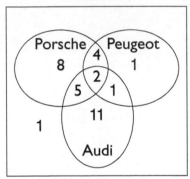

23 How many children like both Audi and Peugeot cars?

A 1   **B** 3   **C** 2   **D** 5   **E** 24

24 Out of all of the children asked, how many do not like Peugeots?

A 24   **B** 13   **C** 25   **D** 16   **E** 12

25 How many children like Porsche cars, but do not like Audi cars?

A 12   **B** 17   **C** 23   **D** 8   **E** 24

CONTINUE WORKING ▶

(26) How many children like all of Porsche, Audi and Peugeot cars?

A   3   **B**   32   **C**   7   **D**   2   **E**   6

(27) How many children like Audi and Peugeot cars, but not Porsche cars?

A   1   **B**   3   **C**   2   **D**   5   **E**   12

(28) Complete the following magic square by choosing the five numbers to go in the place of a, b, c, d and e in the correct order.

Each row, column and diagonal adds up to the same number.

a	b	c
d	e	5
7	1	7

A   3, 9, 3, 5, 3
B   2, 9, 3, 5, 5
C   3, 9, 2, 5, 5
D   3, 9, 3, 3, 5
E   3, 9, 3, 5, 5

(29) A mystery number, p is divided by 10. The result is subtracted from 99. The answer is 89.

Solve the mystery to find the value of p.

A   10   **B**   100   **C**   109   **D**   1   **E**   0

(30) Mike has five times as many marbles as Julia. Julia has the same number of marbles as Mark. There are 91 marbles in total. How many marbles does Mike have?

A   39   **B**   13   **C**   26   **D**   65   **E**   60

(31) Look at the triangle below, which shows the lengths of each side in cm.

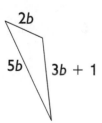

2b

5b   3b + 1

The perimeter = 101 cm. Calculate the value of b.

A   20   **B**   8   **C**   10   **D**   15   **E**   21

CONTINUE WOKING

32 Calculate 17 ÷ 0.15

(Include three digits after the decimal point in your answer.)

A	113.333	B	112.344	C	111.785
D	113.345	E	113.453		

33 A gymnastics club has 43 people inside. There are 14 adults. There are 35 men and children.

Use the information above to calculate the number of men, women and children.

A   Men 6, women 8, children 29
B   Men 6, women 6, children 31
C   Men 6, women 8, children 27
D   Men 5, women 9, children 29
E   Men 8, women 5, children 29

34 How many days are there between the following two dates (including the two dates given).

25th April to 14th June

A	50	B	416	C	51	D	415	E	49

35 The 16.29 coach takes three hours and 45 minutes to arrive at its destination. What time does the coach arrive at its destination?

A	20.04	B	19.29	C	19.14	D	21.11	E	20.14

36 Look at the quadrilateral below and calculate the size of angle *a*.

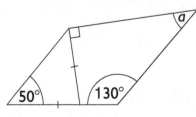

A	65°	B	30°	C	55°	D	80°	E	40°

CONTINUE WORKING ⇨

37 Look at the quadrilateral below and calculate the size of angle *e* (not drawn to scale).

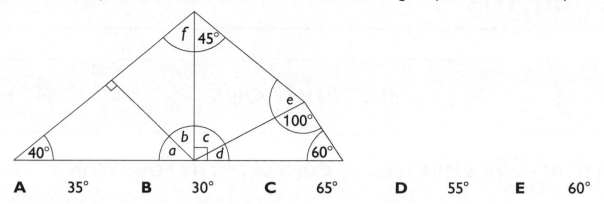

| A | 35° | B | 30° | C | 65° | D | 55° | E | 60° |

38 Look at the following table showing the rate of exchange between the three currencies. Calculate the number that should go in the place of the ?

GB Pounds	Euros	US Dollars
150	165	225
600	660	900
?	1210	1650

A	1,150	B	1,500	C	1,010
D	1,100	E	1,350		

39 I am trying to work out the dimensions of a rectangle. The length is 12 times the width. The perimeter is 104 cm. Calculate the length and width of the rectangle.

A   length 48 cm, width 4 cm
B   length 28 cm, width 24 cm
C   length 20 cm, width 32 cm
D   length 12 cm, width 1 cm
E   length 36 cm, width 3 cm

STOP AND WAIT FOR FURTHER INSTRUCTIONS ⊗

Synonyms

INSTRUCTIONS

 YOU HAVE 5 MINUTES TO COMPLETE THE FOLLOWING SECTION.

YOU HAVE 20 QUESTIONS TO COMPLETE WITHIN THE TIME GIVEN.

EXAMPLES

Select the word that is most similar in meaning to the following word:

cold

A	B	C	D	E
collect	fence	foggy	windy	chilly

The correct answer is E. This has already been marked in Example 1 in the Synonyms section of your answer sheet.

Practice Question 1

Select the word that is most similar in meaning to the following word:

start

A	B	C	D	E
cramped	begin	free	without	change

The correct answer is B. Please mark this in Practice Question 1 in the Synonyms section of your answer sheet.

STOP AND WAIT FOR FURTHER INSTRUCTIONS

In each question, identify the word in the table that is most similar in meaning to the given word.

(1) assure

A	B	C	D	E
strike	verbose	prohibited	detract	guarantee

(2) gracious

A	B	C	D	E
hamlet	pardon	frustration	courteous	stasis

(3) frantic

A	B	C	D	E
frenzied	kingdom	arctic	fleeting	confident

(4) flourish

A	B	C	D	E
glory	perpetuity	illusion	thrive	alliance

(5) fringe

A	B	C	D	E
border	patrol	carousel	amenable	arctic

(6) agility

A	B	C	D	E
contend	impertinent	swathe	pious	nimbleness

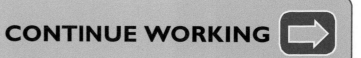

CONTINUE WORKING

7 uncontrollable

A	B	C	D	E
belief	encounter	unruly	pioneer	rant

8 synthetic

A	B	C	D	E
artificial	fearful	drab	convalescence	drawback

9 royal

A	B	C	D	E
imperial	cartographer	vow	fool	penetrate

10 disguise

A	B	C	D	E
extend	liberal	inconspicuous	masquerade	behaviour

11 flexible

A	B	C	D	E
elude	prosperous	undeniable	supple	deliberate

12 twist

A	B	C	D	E
wring	role	terminus	reposition	assortment

13 impartial

A	B	C	D	E
acclimatise	neutral	guile	celebrated	idler

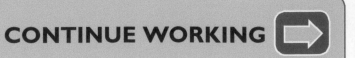

CONTINUE WORKING

14 overhear

A	B	C	D	E
eavesdrop	correct	understandable	desert	haul

15 understand

A	B	C	D	E
leading	pace	comprehend	gratuity	firm

16 attire

A	B	C	D	E
clothing	disorder	apt	psychiatrist	handicap

17 contest

A	B	C	D	E
erratic	oppose	wail	novice	picture

18 enemy

A	B	C	D	E
coast	pompous	enquire	bustling	foe

19 dishonest

A	B	C	D	E
deceitful	unsanitary	persist	arrogant	yield

20 solve

A	B	C	D	E
flaw	phoney	admission	unravel	persist

STOP AND WAIT FOR FURTHER INSTRUCTIONS

Non-Verbal Reasoning

 YOU HAVE 8 MINUTES TO COMPLETE THE FOLLOWING SECTION.

YOU HAVE 9 QUESTIONS TO COMPLETE WITHIN THE TIME GIVEN.

EXAMPLES

COMPLETE THE SEQUENCE Example 1

Select the picture from below that will complete the sequence in place of the ?

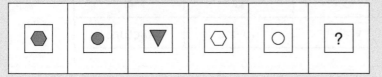

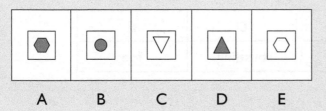

A   B   C   D   E

The correct answer is C. This has already been marked in Example 1 in the Non-Verbal Reasoning section of your answer sheet.

CONTINUE WORKING

COMPLETE THE SEQUENCE Practice Question 1

Select the picture from below that will complete the sequence in place of the ?

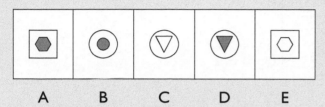

| A | B | C | D | E |

The correct answer is D. Please mark this in Practice Question 1 in the Non-Verbal Reasoning section of your answer sheet.

ROTATION Example 2

Select one of the images below that is a rotation of the image on the left.

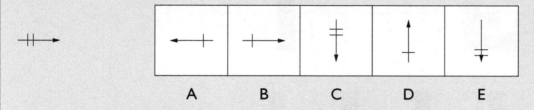

| A | B | C | D | E |

The correct answer is C. This has already been marked in Example 2 in the Non-Verbal Reasoning section of your answer sheet.

ROTATION Practice Question 2

Select one of the images below that is a rotation of the image on the left.

 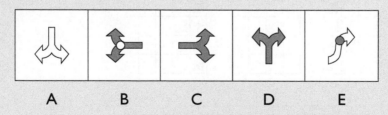

| A | B | C | D | E |

The correct answer is B. Please mark this in Practice Question 2 in the Non-Verbal Reasoning section of your answer sheet.

STOP AND WAIT FOR FURTHER INSTRUCTIONS ⊗

Select the pictures which will complete the following sequence:

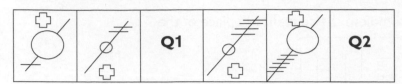

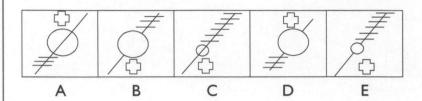

A   B   C   D   E

(1) Select the picture you think should go in place of Q1 here.

(2) Select the picture you think should go in place of Q2 here.

(3) Which pattern completes the sequence in place of the blank grid below?

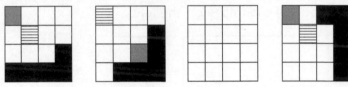

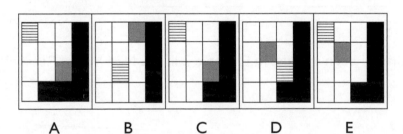

A   B   C   D   E

(4) Which pattern completes the sequence in place of the blank grid below?

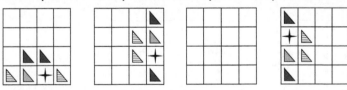

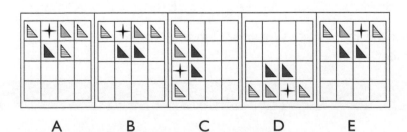

A   B   C   D   E

CONTINUE WORKING

(5) Which shape or pattern completes the larger square?

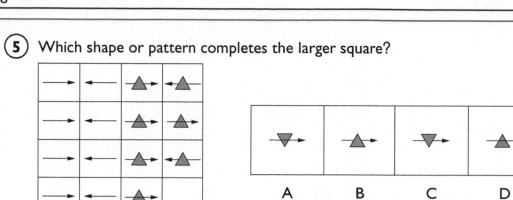

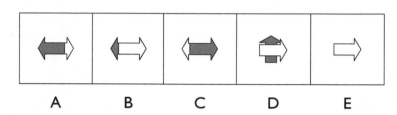

(6) Which shape or pattern completes the larger square?

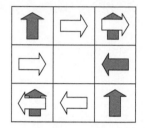

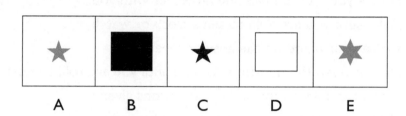

(7) Which shape or pattern completes the larger square?

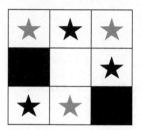

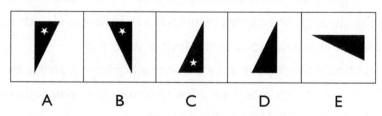

(8) Select one of the images below that is a rotation of the image on the left.

(9) Select one of the images below that is a rotation of the image on the left.

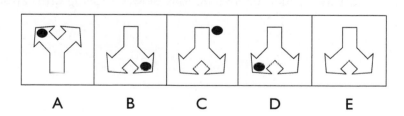

END OF PAPER

Test C Paper 2

Instructions

1. Ensure you have pencils and an eraser with you.
2. Make sure you are able to see a clock or watch.
3. Write your name on the answer sheet.
4. Do not open the question booklet until you are told to do so by the audio instructions.
5. Listen carefully to the audio instructions given.
6. Mark your answers on the answer sheet only.
7. All workings must be completed on a separate piece of paper.
8. You should not use a calculator, dictionary or thesaurus at any point in this paper.
9. Move through the papers as quickly as possible and with care.
10. Follow the instructions at the foot of each page.
11. You should mark your answers with a horizontal strike, as shown on the answer sheet.
12. If you want to change your answer, ensure that you rub out your first answer and that your second answer is clearly more visible.
13. You can go back and review any questions that are within the section you are working on only. You must await further instructions before moving onto another section.

Symbols and Phrases used in the Tests

 Instructions    Time allowed for this section   Stop and wait for further instructions   Continue working

Cloze Sentences

INSTRUCTIONS

 YOU HAVE 7 MINUTES TO COMPLETE THE FOLLOWING SECTION.

YOU HAVE 17 QUESTIONS TO COMPLETE WITHIN THE TIME GIVEN.

EXAMPLES

Example 1

Complete the sentence in the most sensible way by selecting the appropriate word from each set of brackets.

The (dog, big, gate) sat on the (mat, open, great).

A   big, open
B   dog, great
C   gate, mat
D   dog, mat
E   dog, open

The correct answer is D. This has already been marked in Example 1 of the Cloze Sentences section of your answer sheet.

Practice Question 1

Complete the sentence in the most sensible way by selecting the appropriate word from each set of brackets.

My name is (Helen, high, sand) and I am (ten, dig, land) years old.

A   Helen, dig
B   high, land
C   sand, land
D   Helen, land
E   Helen, ten

The correct answer is E. Please mark the answer E in Practice Question 1 in the Cloze Sentences section of your answer sheet.

CONTINUE WORKING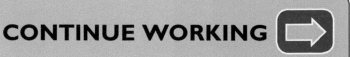

Example 2

One word in the following sentence has had three letters removed from it. Keeping the letters in the same order, identify the three-letter word that is made from these missing letters.

The pupil could not pay attion.

The correct answer is 'ten'. This is shown in Example 2 in the Cloze Sentences section of your answer sheet.

Practice Question 2

One word in the following sentence has had three letters removed from it. Keeping the letters in the same order, identify the three-letter word that is made from these missing letters.

She treasu her mother's bracelet.

The correct answer is 'red'. Please write this in Practice Question 2 in the Cloze Sentences section of your answer sheet.

STOP AND WAIT FOR FURTHER INSTRUCTIONS

Complete the most sensible sentence by selecting the appropriate combination of words from within the brackets. Use one word from each set of brackets.

(1) The (plumber, dentist, butcher) took time to reassure me before starting work on my (garden, teeth, hair).

    A   plumber, teeth
    B   butcher, hair
    C   butcher, garden
    D   dentist, teeth
    E   dentist, garden

(2) (Despite, Hence, During) the shortfall in numbers, a good (time, weather, seasonal) was had by all (art, rent, guests).

    A   Hence, time, rent
    B   During, time, art
    C   Despite, time, guests
    D   Despite, weather, guests
    E   During, time, rent

CONTINUE WORKING

(3) They were hoping the (sympathetic, weather, yesterday) would be better than it had been (recently, tomorrow, treasured).

- **A**   yesterday, treasured
- **B**   weather, recently
- **C**   yesterday, tomorrow
- **D**   sympathetic, recently
- **E**   weather, treasured

(4) The (support, troubles, health) of the (airport, dream, nation) was behind the athletes.

- **A**   troubles, nation
- **B**   troubles, airport
- **C**   support, nation
- **D**   health, dream
- **E**   troubles, dream

(5) The (depth, puppy, temperature) of (sympathy, pool, horses) was very much appreciated by the mourners.

- **A**   depth, pool
- **B**   temperature, pool
- **C**   puppy, horses
- **D**   depth, sympathy
- **E**   depth, horses

(6) The (internet, tortoise, ambulance) rushed to the (scene, clouds, music).

- **A**   internet, music
- **B**   tortoise, scene
- **C**   ambulance, scene
- **D**   internet, clouds
- **E**   ambulance, clouds

(7) (Where, When, Who) would arrive first was anybody's (dress, guess, blessed).

- **A**   Where, blessed
- **B**   Who, dress
- **C**   When, dress
- **D**   Who, guess
- **E**   Where, guess

CONTINUE WORKING ⇨

(8) The (underneath, ultimate, outcome) of the court case was due (imminently, window, grass).

A underneath, imminently
B ultimate, grass
C outcome, imminently
D underneath, grass
E ultimate, window

(9) The (monkey, bungalow, empathy) perched on her shoulder and (rug, hastened, smiled) for the (chair, camera, sun).

A empathy, smiled, camera
B bungalow, hastened, sun
C empathy, rug, chair
D monkey, smiled, camera
E monkey, rug, sun

(10) How the (direction, completeness, magician) managed to do that, I will (endeavour, never, have) know!

A direction, have
B completeness, have
C magician, never
D magician, have
E completeness, endeavour

One word in the following sentence has had three letters removed from it. Keeping the letters in the same order, identify the three-letter word that is made from these three missing letters.

(11) The flowers were attracg the butterflies.

(12) The instabiy of the suspension bridge meant closure was the only option.

(13) The pocopier had run out of paper.

(14) They were feeling confit as they set out on their expedition.

(15) They enjoyed dling their feet in the sea on the hot summer's day.

(16) They decided to meet up the foling month.

(17) ry little detail had been considered.

STOP AND WAIT FOR FURTHER INSTRUCTIONS

Problem Solving

INSTRUCTIONS

 YOU HAVE 12 MINUTES TO COMPLETE THE FOLLOWING SECTION.

YOU HAVE 10 QUESTIONS TO COMPLETE WITHIN THE TIME GIVEN.

EXAMPLES

A	£2.60	B	£3.40	C	£2.40	D	25	E	£1.35
F	£3.40	G	14	H	31	I	28	J	34

Example 1

Calculate the following:

If I buy five apples at 20p each, and four bananas at 35p each, how much change will I receive if I pay with a £5 note.

The correct answer is A. This has already been marked in Example 1 in the Problem Solving section of your answer sheet.

Practice Question 1

Calculate the following:

There are 17 people on a bus when it arrives at a bus stop. Eleven people get on the bus, and three get off. How many people are then left on the bus?

The correct answer is D. Please mark this in Practice Question 1 in the Problem Solving section of your answer sheet.

STOP AND WAIT FOR FURTHER INSTRUCTIONS

A	53	B	12	C	£527	D	£52	E	£41.40
F	5	G	9	H	10	I	27	J	£35.00

Read the passage below, then select an answer to each question from the 10 different possible answers in the table above. You may use an answer for more than one question.

Sarah is a pupil at Woodbridge Middle School. There are four girls to every five boys in her class. There are 15 boys in Sarah's class.

Sarah's brother Sam attends the same school and Sam is 4 now. In two years' time, Sarah will be twice as old as her brother Sam.

The number of children that attend the school has grown over the last few years, as a new development of houses was recently built in the area. There are now around 150 pupils in the school. There are 76 children in years 4, 5 and 6 combined.

Every year the school raises money for a charity. Sarah is collecting money for the charity from her class, and has completed a sponsored walk. All of the pupils in her class donated £1, except two children who gave £2 each, and six children who donated £5 each. Sarah did not donate any money.

As the number of pupils attending Woodbridge Middle School is growing, the school governors have decided to improve the school by building new classrooms, and refreshing the current classrooms. Sarah's classroom requires a new floor. The dimensions of the floor are 8 m by 4 m. Most of the improvements to the school are being completed at the weekends when the school is always closed.

Part of the money to improve the school is being raised from an increase in the cost of school lunches for the children. These increased by 20p on Wednesday 1st March to £1.80.

Also, in order to raise money, the class organised a raffle for the school fete. A number of prizes were donated, and there was also a special cash prize of £100. The £100 was allocated from the money raised from selling raffle tickets. Ticket sales were as follows:

123 books of tickets were sold at £5 per book.

60 individual tickets were also sold at 20p per ticket.

(1) How many children are there in Sarah's class?

(2) How old is Sarah now?

(3) If there are 23 children in Year 5, how many children are there in years 4 and 6 combined?

CONTINUE WORKING

(4) How much did Sarah raise for charity from her class?

(5) If the tiles used to cover the floor in Sarah's classroom are 50 cm by 50 cm, and come in boxes of 15, how many boxes of tiles are required to cover the entire floor?

(6) Sarah has added up all of the girls' shoe sizes, and they total 60. What is the mean shoe size of the girls in Sarah's class?

(7) How much does Sarah spend on her lunch in March, if she is not absent for any of the school days?

(8) The school buys plastic cups in tubes of 200. If 10 cups cost 3.5p, how much do 50 tubes of plastic cups cost?

(9) In school assembly one morning, there are 174 people in the room. Of these people:

- boys and teachers make up 99 people

- girls and teachers make up 87 people.

How many teachers are in the room?

(10) How much was raised by the raffle after all the prizes were claimed?

STOP AND WAIT FOR FURTHER INSTRUCTIONS

Antonyms

 YOU HAVE 10 MINUTES TO COMPLETE THE FOLLOWING SECTION.

YOU HAVE 25 QUESTIONS TO COMPLETE WITHIN THE TIME GIVEN.

EXAMPLES

Example 1

Which word is least similar to the following word:

light

A	B	C	D	E
dark	water	feather	bright	hill

The correct answer is A. This has already been marked in Example 1 in the Antonyms section of your answer sheet.

Practice Question 1

Which word is least similar to the following word:

smooth

A	B	C	D	E
allow	beneath	rough	whilst	shade

The correct answer is C. Please mark the answer C in Practice Question 1 in the Antonyms section of your answer sheet.

STOP AND WAIT FOR FURTHER INSTRUCTIONS

Which word is least similar to the following word:

(1) fresh

A	B	C	D	E
board	stale	silence	increase	indeed

(2) stationary

A	B	C	D	E
unsurprised	phone	perilous	mobile	paper

(3) steep

A	B	C	D	E
home	reject	bold	separate	gradual

(4) straight

A	B	C	D	E
crooked	merry	bright	gentle	success

(5) superior

A	B	C	D	E
contaminated	silence	dull	inferior	shrink

(6) tame

A	B	C	D	E
prohibit	sweet	wild	preserve	modest

CONTINUE WORKING ⇨

(7) tiny

A	B	C	D	E
fade	incompetent	decrease	enormous	advance

(8) unite

A	B	C	D	E
separate	imprudent	selfish	absurd	follower

(9) vacant

A	B	C	D	E
height	relaxed	unfriendly	occupied	disperse

(10) clear

A	B	C	D	E
reduce	valour	sober	fondness	vague

(11) better

A	B	C	D	E
fade	generous	genuine	reaction	worse

(12) combine

A	B	C	D	E
contract	separate	fertile	loose	crooked

(13) encourage

A	B	C	D	E
courage	impolite	guilty	discourage	mild

CONTINUE WORKING ▶

14 import

A	B	C	D	E
strict	cavity	indirect	legal	export

15 brighten

A	B	C	D	E
fade	trick	delight	stale	disobedient

16 boundless

A	B	C	D	E
limited	gradual	admit	increase	occupied

17 decrease

A	B	C	D	E
admiration	separate	increase	abundant	genuine

18 admit

A	B	C	D	E
fail	mobile	legal	immigration	deny

19 action

A	B	C	D	E
displeasure	constant	inaction	loose	often

CONTINUE WORKING ⇨

20 enigmatic

A	B	C	D	E
clear	graceful	innocent	minute	ally

21 changeable

A	B	C	D	E
allay	separate	constant	imprudent	smart

22 pleasure

A	B	C	D	E
fail	encouraged	simple	disperse	displeasure

23 order

A	B	C	D	E
hinder	bright	stale	singular	disorder

24 amateur

A	B	C	D	E
modern	professional	usual	disloyal	cramped

25 domestic

A	B	C	D	E
foreign	mobile	introvert	mild	shrink

STOP AND WAIT FOR FURTHER INSTRUCTIONS ⬡✕

Non-Verbal Reasoning

  INSTRUCTIONS

YOU HAVE 8 MINUTES TO COMPLETE THE FOLLOWING SECTION.

YOU HAVE 15 QUESTIONS TO COMPLETE WITHIN THE TIME GIVEN.

EXAMPLES

CODES Example 1

Look at the codes for the following patterns and identify the missing code for the pattern on the far right.

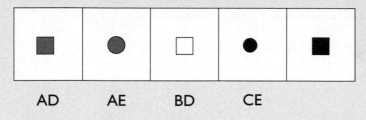

A	BE
B	AD
C	BC
D	BD
E	CD

The correct answer is E. This has already been marked in Example 1 in the Non-Verbal Reasoning section of your answer sheet.

CODES Practice Question 1

Look at the codes for the following patterns and identify the missing code for the pattern on the far right.

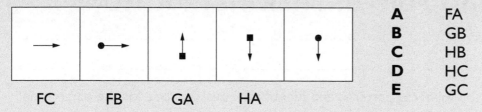

A	FA
B	GB
C	HB
D	HC
E	GC

The correct answer is C. Please mark this in Practice Question 1 in the Non-Verbal Reasoning section of your answer sheet.

CONTINUE WORKING ⬛

COMPLETE THE SQUARE Example 2

Which shape or pattern completes the square?

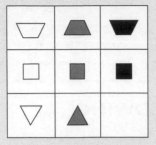

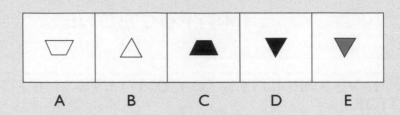

The correct answer is D. This has already been marked in Example 2 in the Non-Verbal Reasoning section of your answer sheet.

COMPLETE THE SQUARE Practice Question 2

Which shape or pattern completes the square?

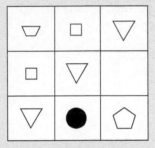

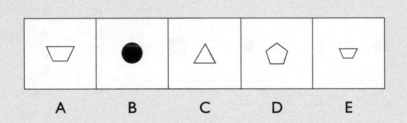

The correct answer is B. Please mark this in Practice Question 2 in the Non-Verbal Reasoning section of your answer sheet.

STOP AND WAIT FOR FURTHER INSTRUCTIONS

1 Look at the codes for the following patterns and identify the missing code for the pattern on the far right.

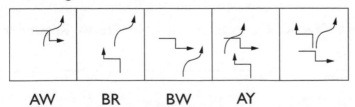

AW   BR   BW   AY

A	BY
B	AR
C	AY
D	BW
E	BR

CONTINUE WORKING

(2) Look at the codes for the following patterns and identify the missing code for the pattern on the far right.

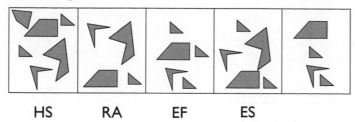

	HS	RA	EF	ES

A   EF
B   RF
C   RA
D   RS
E   EA

(3) Look at the codes for the following patterns and identify the missing code for the pattern on the far right.

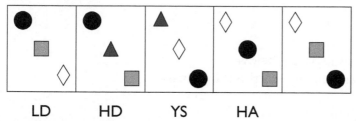

	LD	HD	YS	HA

A   LH
B   HD
C   LB
D   YS
E   YA

(4) Look at the codes for the following patterns and identify the missing code for the pattern on the far right.

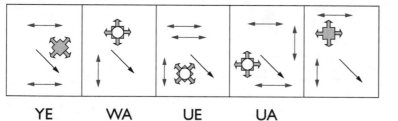

	YE	WA	UE	UA

A   WA
B   YA
C   WE
D   UA
E   YE

(5) Look at the two shapes on the left immediately below.
Find the connection between them and apply it to the third shape.

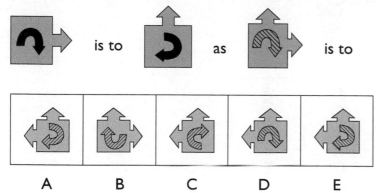

A	B	C	D	E

CONTINUE WORKING

(6) Look at the two shapes on the left immediately below.
Find the connection between them and apply it to the third shape.

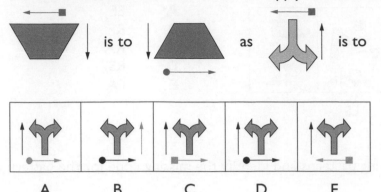

| A | B | C | D | E |

(7) Look at the two shapes on the left immediately below.
Find the connection between them and apply it to the third shape.

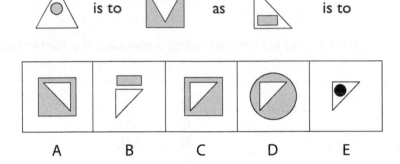

| A | B | C | D | E |

(8) Look at the two shapes on the left immediately below.
Find the connection between them and apply it to the third shape.

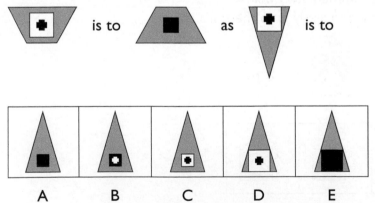

| A | B | C | D | E |

CONTINUE WORKING ⇨

9 Select the correct picture from the bottom row in order to finish the incomplete sequence on the top row.

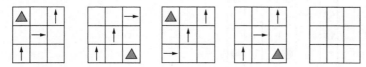

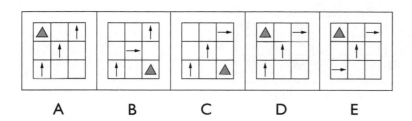

A   B   C   D   E

10 Select the picture from below that will complete the sequence in place of the?

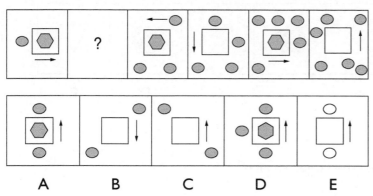

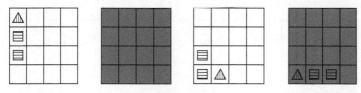

A   B   C   D   E

11 Which pattern completes the sequence in place of the blank grid below?

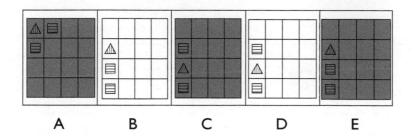

A   B   C   D   E

CONTINUE WORKING

12 Which pattern completes the sequence in place of the blank grid below?

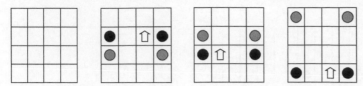

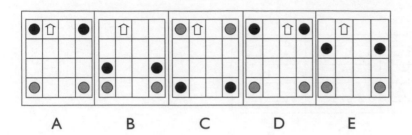

A   B   C   D   E

13 Which shape or pattern completes the larger square?

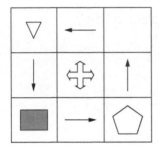

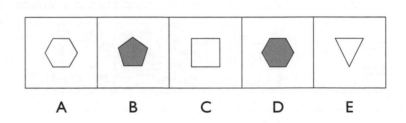

A   B   C   D   E

14 Which shape or pattern completes the larger square?

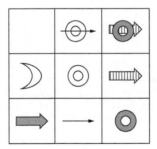

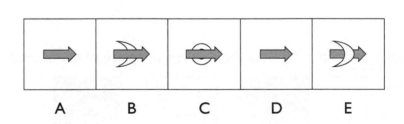

A   B   C   D   E

15 Which shape or pattern completes the larger square?

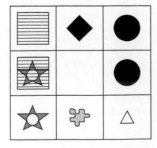

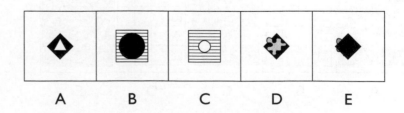

A   B   C   D   E

STOP AND WAIT FOR FURTHER INSTRUCTIONS ⊗

Shuffled Sentences

INSTRUCTIONS

 YOU HAVE 8 MINUTES TO COMPLETE THE FOLLOWING SECTION.

YOU HAVE 15 QUESTIONS TO COMPLETE WITHIN THE TIME GIVEN.

EXAMPLES

Example 1

The following sentence is shuffled and also contains one unnecessary word. Rearrange the sentence correctly, in order to identify the unnecessary word.

dog the ran fetch the to stick gluing.

A	B	C	D	E
gluing	dog	ran	the	stick

The correct answer is A. This has already been marked in Example 1 in the Shuffled Sentences section of your answer sheet.

Practice Question 1

The following sentence is shuffled and also contains one unnecessary word. Rearrange the sentence correctly, in order to identify the unnecessary word.

pushed Emma stood up and closed the table under the chairs.

A	B	C	D	E
chairs	stood	under	closed	Emma

The correct answer is D. Please mark this in Practice Question 1 in the Shuffled Sentences section of your answer sheet.

STOP AND WAIT FOR FURTHER INSTRUCTIONS

The following sentence is shuffled and also contains one unnecessary word. Rearrange the sentence correctly, in order to identify the unnecessary word.

① a strewn streets was night's the neighbourhood's across storm of last result debris as an.

A	B	C	D	E
an	night's	result	debris	strewn

② airport delays caused the bad weather to severe whether flights at the.

A	B	C	D	E
whether	bad	flights	airport	severe

③ this big difference is likely to make those a.

A	B	C	D	E
difference	likely	big	those	this

④ the leaf in the tree decided to she through book bookshop whilst.

A	B	C	D	E
tree	through	whilst	decided	book

⑤ although it was now the parents of the responsibility.

A	B	C	D	E
it	now	parents	although	responsibility

⑥ checked all the scores there were confirm to their accuracy.

A	B	C	D	E
were	there	accuracy	confirm	scores

CONTINUE WORKING

7 seen she by what was she had scene astounded just.

A	B	C	D	E
she	astounded	scene	what	was

8 the ideal central location was mirrored for them.

A	B	C	D	E
them	central	ideal	mirrored	the

9 was the hallway positioned in the hanging basket.

A	B	C	D	E
hanging	was	in	hallway	the

10 to recover the several attempts were made cargo sunk.

A	B	C	D	E
attempts	sunk	recover	cargo	made

11 the journey taken car hours by three took.

A	B	C	D	E
car	journey	took	taken	hours

12 the ball dress kicked code stipulated for annual formal the attire charity.

A	B	C	D	E
kicked	ball	stipulated	charity	formal

13 provided the storage chest bedroom drawers waist extra of in the.

A	B	C	D	E
waist	drawers	extra	storage	of

CONTINUE WORKING

14 must use the theatre prohibited of was cameras in.

A	B	C	D	E
prohibited	use	theatre	must	cameras

15 was in accept a payment return for cash offered discount in.

A	B	C	D	E
discount	accept	cash	in	for

END OF PAPER

Test D Paper 1

Instructions

1. Ensure you have pencils and an eraser with you.
2. Make sure you are able to see a clock or watch.
3. Write your name on the answer sheet.
4. Do not open the question booklet until you are told to do so by the audio instructions.
5. Listen carefully to the audio instructions given.
6. Mark your answers on the answer sheet only.
7. All workings must be completed on a separate piece of paper.
8. You should not use a calculator, dictionary or thesaurus at any point in this paper.
9. Move through the papers as quickly as possible and with care.
10. Follow the instructions at the foot of each page.
11. You should mark your answers with a horizontal strike, as shown on the answer sheet.
12. If you want to change your answer, ensure that you rub out your first answer and that your second answer is clearly more visible.
13. You can go back and review any questions that are within the section you are working on only. You must await further instructions before moving onto another section.

Symbols and Phrases used in the Tests

 Instructions   Time allowed for this section   Stop and wait for further instructions   Continue working

Comprehension

 YOU HAVE 10 MINUTES TO COMPLETE THE FOLLOWING SECTION.

YOU HAVE 10 QUESTIONS TO COMPLETE WITHIN THE TIME GIVEN.

EXAMPLES

Comprehension Example

Some people choose to start their Christmas shopping early in October. It has been reported that some people even buy their Christmas presents in the sales in August. In recent years, people have the option of purchasing their Christmas presents online.

Example 1

According to the passage, what is the earliest that people start their Christmas shopping?

A   In the preceding summer
B   In the preceding October
C   In the preceding November
D   Christmas Eve
E   In early December

The correct answer is A. This has already been marked in Example 1 in the Comprehension section of your answer sheet.

Practice Question 1

In recent years, what has caused a change in how people shop?

A   There are more shops
B   Shops are more crowded
C   You can easily organise your journey to the shops
D   New products are available
E   There has been a rise in use of the Internet

The correct answer is E. Please mark this in Practice Question 1 in the Comprehension section of your answer sheet.

STOP AND WAIT FOR FURTHER INSTRUCTIONS

Read the following passage, then answer the questions below.

A Perspective on the Changing World of Communication

Communication has developed over the millennia at a phenomenal rate. It continues to develop and, as a result, the world has become unrecognisable for many older people.

Communication is made up of verbal communication (spoken), non-verbal communication (body language) and the written word.

Face-to-face communication is complex and subtle messages are often conveyed through body language and eye movements. Many people now study these signs to learn how to read the signals that the person is unintentionally giving away, rather than just listening to the words which are being spoken. People wish to master these signals to enhance their business skills and to assist their career path. People also study this for interpersonal relations outside of the business environment.

Interpreting signals from body language seems quite the opposite of communication via emails and texts, which do not have the benefit of facial expressions and body language to help convey the right message. The tone of emails can easily be misconstrued. When writing an email, it is very important to choose words carefully and read the whole email to check how the email will be interpreted by the recipient. To reintroduce some sort of human emotion, many people also include icons or 'emoticons' in their texts and emails, such as a 'smiley face'. Instantly, the recipient is given the message that this email or text has happy and informal content.

In the context of the business world, emails have drastically reduced the time it takes to communicate to large numbers of people within an organisation, or between organisations. Teams of people can easily be brought together for a meeting via video calls, often saving a huge amount of time and money on travel. The decisions and actions which are a result of these meetings, the 'Minutes', can be communicated easily, cheaply and quickly. In the business environment, icons are inappropriate and should be avoided.

Many people now receive so many emails that it is unmanageable to read and respond to the vast majority of them. As people receive so many emails, many remain unread and are simply deleted. As people become aware that the detail in emails is often skimmed over, people's communication styles have changed. It is advised that lengthy emails should be avoided, unless it is absolutely necessary to write more.

People are now almost always contactable by phone and it is hard to think that just over thirty years ago the first commercially available mobile phones were the size of a household brick and limited to phone calls only. Since then, the size of mobile phones has reduced and the tasks which can be performed on them have broadened. People are able to run their social lives as well as their business lives via 'apps', which is the shortened word for 'applications'. It could be said that people now communicate less by phone, as many would prefer to text or communicate via social media.

CONTINUE WORKING

How different the world is now. A person born in the early to mid-20th century has seen so many fundamental changes in the world, that it has become unrecognisable. Many elderly people find that communicating using today's technology is out of this world and incomprehensible; whereas technology is the norm to most young people. There are now many initiatives which seek to assist elderly people to understand how to use the Internet. Subsequently, elderly people can then learn how to use social media to keep them in touch with their families. In addition, they can complete tasks such as online shopping, online banking and memory games.

(1) What signals are important in face-to-face communication?

A   The spoken word only
B   The written word
C   Body language and eye movements
D   Signals written on the wall
E   Emails only

(2) Why do people study body language for business purposes?

A   To be able to understand what people are saying
B   To make their emails more coherent
C   To understand foreign languages
D   To enhance interpersonal relationships
E   To further their career and to bring them success

(3) What is the meaning of 'misconstrued'?

A   Miscalculated
B   Misdial
C   Misunderstood
D   Mislead
E   Misbehaved

(4) According to the passage, what are the benefits of email communication regarding meetings?

A   The meetings have to be attended by many people
B   The meetings are shorter
C   The details from the meetings are instantly recorded
D   The details from the meetings can be easily sent to a significant amount of people
E   The details from the meetings can be typed up easily

CONTINUE WORKING

(5) According to the passage, which phrase below best describes how mobile phones have developed?

A   Mobiles phones are now often used in business meetings
B   The size of mobile phones has reduced and their capabilities have increased
C   Mobile phones have not dramatically changed or developed
D   Mobile phones have replaced verbal communication
E   The size of mobile phones has reduced and the use of them is limited

(6) According to the passage, what often happens to emails which are received?

A   A large number of emails are unread or deleted
B   Almost all emails are read and responded to
C   Very few emails are deleted
D   Many emails are forwarded to large amounts of people
E   Many emails are lengthy and are always read

(7) In the context of the passage, what type of word is 'household'?

A   Noun
B   Adjective
C   Verb
D   Pronoun
E   Adverb

(8) What is the meaning of 'commonplace'?

A   A place that everyone knows
B   An item that is low in quality
C   An item that people use in their everyday life
D   An item that is rarely used
E   An item that is easy to understand

(9) In the context of the passage, which of the words below is the opposite of 'incomprehensible'?

A   User-friendly
B   Unfriendly
C   Unintelligible
D   Compatible
E   Sensible

(10) Which phrase best describes the final paragraph in the passage?

A   Elderly people understand the changes in technology
B   Most elderly people use social media daily
C   Elderly people are being taught how to communicate via social media
D   Many young people are teaching elderly people how to use the Internet
E   Elderly people are being taught the dangers of social media

STOP AND WAIT FOR FURTHER INSTRUCTIONS

Numeracy

INSTRUCTIONS

 YOU HAVE 17 MINUTES TO COMPLETE THE FOLLOWING SECTION.

YOU HAVE 28 QUESTIONS TO COMPLETE WITHIN THE TIME GIVEN.

EXAMPLES

Example 1

Calculate 53 – 42

A   12   **B**   1   **C**   4   **D**   5   **E**   11

The correct answer is E. This has already been marked in Example 1 in the Numeracy section of your answer sheet.

Practice Question 1

Calculate 95 – 75

A   21   **B**   20   **C**   19   **D**   18   **E**   13

The correct answer is B. Please mark this in Practice Question 1 in the Numeracy section of your answer sheet.

STOP AND WAIT FOR FURTHER INSTRUCTIONS

(1) 36,048 ÷ 12

    A   3,040   **B**   304   **C**   4,003   **D**   3,004   **E**   34

(2) $12^2 - 11^2$

    A   144   **B**   23   **C**   133   **D**   10   **E**   165

③ $\frac{1}{3}$ of 294

A   102   **B**   97   **C**   96   **D**   9   **E**   98

④ What is the size of each interior angle in a pentagon?

A   72°   **B**   62°   **C**   105°   **D**   108°   **E**   150°

⑤ Find a, if $b = 2a - 4$ and $b = 4$

A   0   **B**   8   **C**   4   **D**   2   **E**   1

⑥ If $b = 8$, find a using the following equation:

$8a - b = 0$

A   8   **B**   2   **C**   0   **D**   1   **E**   4

⑦ Find the missing number marked by?

$5 \times 3 + ? = 20$

A   1   **B**   5   **C**   4   **D**   17   **E**   10

⑧ Find the missing number marked by?

$8 \times ? - 8 = 72$

A   1   **B**   10   **C**   5   **D**   8   **E**   17

⑨ Find the missing number marked by?

$? + 5 \times 3 = 30$

A   1   **B**   5   **C**   2   **D**   4   **E**   15

⑩ If wrapping paper costs £1.50 per metre, how many rolls can I buy for £10? Each roll is 3 m long.

A   6   **B**   3   **C**   2   **D**   15   **E**   30

CONTINUE WORKING

11 I have just rolled a 4 on a die. The die is a fair die with 6 sides.

What is the probability that the next time I roll the die, I will roll a 4?

A	1 in 4	B	1 in 3	C	1 in 16
D	1 in 36	E	1 in 6		

12 Calculate the answer to the following:

(25 ÷ 5) + 22 − 11 = ?

A	16	B	38	C	27	D	6	E	15

13 I am sharing out a large pizza between guests at a party. There are 20 guests. A quarter of the guests have said they would not like any pizza. The pizza is cut into equal sized slices. A third of the guests who wanted pizza did not have time to eat their pizza. How many pieces of pizza are remaining?

A	4	B	5	C	7	D	6	E	10

14 What is the first number in this sequence marked by ?

? , 29, 24, 20, 17, 15

A	34	B	33	C	35	D	28	E	31

15 What is half of 52?

A	25	B	24	C	26	D	31	E	35

16 I have 56 sweets that I am sharing out equally amongst my 6 friends and myself. How many 7s can I take away from 56?

A	7	B	8	C	6	D	5	E	10

17 The news headlines are repeated on a television channel precisely every 15 minutes. How many times are the headlines shown on the television channel each day?

A	144	B	95	C	40	D	96	E	48

CONTINUE WORKING ⏩

18 What is the next number in the sequence?

0.1, 0.2, 0.4, 0.8, ?

| **A** | 1.6 | **B** | 0.16 | **C** | 0.10 | **D** | 0.12 | **E** | 0.18 |

19 Which amount is largest?

A one-quarter of 124
B one-fifth of 160
C one-tenth of 315
D half of 62
E one-third of 94

20 There are five people in a room. After a while, three of the people leave the room and a further seven people enter the room. How many people are now in the room?

| **A** | 5 | **B** | 3 | **C** | 4 | **D** | 7 | **E** | 9 |

The following three questions relate to the chart shown below:

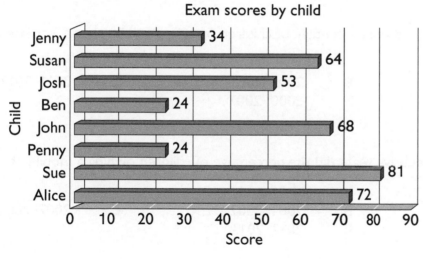

Exam scores by child

21 What is the range?

| **A** | 24 | **B** | 52 | **C** | 35 | **D** | 57 | **E** | 81 |

22 What is the mean exam score?

| **A** | 52.5 | **B** | 55 | **C** | 50 | **D** | 24 | **E** | 81 |

CONTINUE WORKING

(23) What is the median exam score?

| A | 56 | B | 81 | C | 58.5 | D | 54 | E | 35 |

The following five questions relate to the chart shown below:

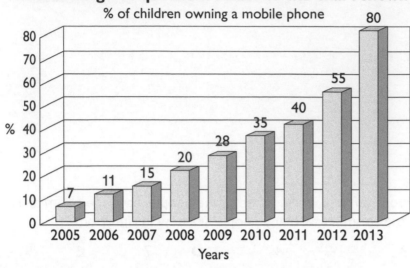

% of children owning a mobile phone

(24) What percentage of children owned a mobile phone in the year 2011?

| A | 25 | B | 35 | C | 40 | D | 20 | E | 15 |

(25) Between which two years did the percentage of children owning a mobile phone increase by five times exactly?

| A | 2006–2012 | B | 2005–2009 | C | 2011–2013 |
| D | 2008–2013 | E | 2000–2007 | | |

(26) Between which two consecutive years did the percentage of children owning a mobile phone increase the most?

| A | 2004–2005 | B | 2001–2002 | C | 2007–2008 |
| D | 2009–2010 | E | 2012–2013 | | |

(27) Calculate the mean percentage of children owning a mobile phone over the period shown.

| A | 31 | B | 34 | C | 32 and $\frac{1}{3}$ |
| D | 23 and $\frac{1}{4}$ | E | 25 and $\frac{1}{5}$ | | |

(28) If the mean percentage of children owning a mobile phone increases to 38 over the period to 2014 (from 2005), what is the percentage of children who owned a mobile phone in 2014?

| A | 65 | B | 60 | C | 75 | D | 89 | E | 100 |

STOP AND WAIT FOR FURTHER INSTRUCTIONS

Synonyms

INSTRUCTIONS

 YOU HAVE 9 MINUTES TO COMPLETE THE FOLLOWING SECTION.

YOU HAVE 20 QUESTIONS TO COMPLETE WITHIN THE TIME GIVEN.

EXAMPLES

Example 1

Select the word that is most similar in meaning to the following word:

cold

A	B	C	D	E
collect	fence	foggy	windy	chilly

The correct answer is E. This has already been marked in Example 1 in the Synonyms section of your answer sheet.

Practice Question 1

Select the word that is most similar in meaning to the following word:

start

A	B	C	D	E
cramped	begin	free	without	change

The correct answer is B. Please mark this in Practice Question 1 in the Synonyms section of your answer sheet.

STOP AND WAIT FOR FURTHER INSTRUCTIONS

In each row, identify the word in the table that is most similar in meaning to the word above the table.

1 daily

A	B	C	D	E
irregularly	routinely	seldom	momentous	calmly

2 falsify

A	B	C	D	E
verify	rectify	easily	distort	validate

3 vigour

A	B	C	D	E
vitality	lethargy	apathy	balanced	caged

4 blossom

A	B	C	D	E
notion	infer	fritter	crazed	unfold

5 recollect

A	B	C	D	E
dial	remember	perverse	despise	recourse

6 organisation

A	B	C	D	E
intermittent	company	alcove	consensus	arrested

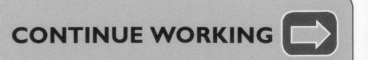

CONTINUE WORKING

7 vintage

A	B	C	D	E
misshapen	advantageous	classic	inopportune	contemporary

8 disclosure

A	B	C	D	E
hone	tumbler	pious	shifting	admission

9 energetic

A	B	C	D	E
multitude	spirited	passive	insolent	motionless

10 thanks

A	B	C	D	E
restless	denial	emptiness	gratitude	anomaly

11 hasten

A	B	C	D	E
hurry	improvement	dawdle	periodic	beautiful

12 quantity

A	B	C	D	E
thoughtless	conviction	delightful	averse	amount

13 ravage

A	B	C	D	E
entail	devour	sustenance	revelry	triumph

CONTINUE WORKING

14 sophisticated

A	B	C	D	E
squalid	derogatory	deplorable	reluctant	civilised

15 genial

A	B	C	D	E
genius	detract	unhappy	detestable	happy

16 radiate

A	B	C	D	E
bard	emanate	aligned	deduce	foolish

17 courteous

A	B	C	D	E
enshroud	affray	polite	pliable	suggest

18 serene

A	B	C	D	E
rounded	glaring	pomp	tranquil	honour

19 diminish

A	B	C	D	E
nifty	lessen	increase	equality	lesson

20 course

A	B	C	D	E
glut	attentive	series	sterile	affectionate

STOP AND WAIT FOR FURTHER INSTRUCTIONS

Non-Verbal Reasoning

 YOU HAVE 9 MINUTES TO COMPLETE THE FOLLOWING SECTION.

YOU HAVE 15 QUESTIONS TO COMPLETE WITHIN THE TIME GIVEN.

EXAMPLES

REFLECTION Example 1

Select an image from the row below that shows how the following shape or pattern will appear when reflected.

The correct answer is E. This has already been marked in Example 1 in the Non-Verbal Reasoning section of your answer sheet.

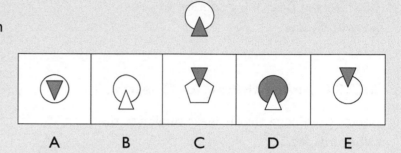

REFLECTION Practice Question 1

Select an image from the row below that shows how the following shape or pattern will appear when reflected.

The correct answer is C. Please mark this in Practice Question 1 in the Non-Verbal Reasoning section of your answer sheet.

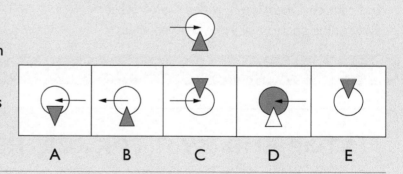

ROTATION Example 2

Select an image from the row below that is a rotation of the following image.

The correct answer is C. This has already been marked in Example 2 in the Non-Verbal Reasoning section of your answer sheet.

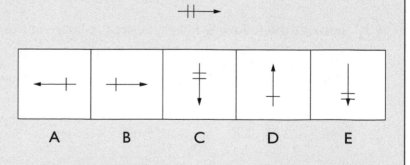

CONTINUE WORKING

ROTATION Practice Question 2

Select an image from the row below that is a rotation of the following image.

The correct answer is B. Please mark this in Practice Question 2 in the Non-Verbal Reasoning section of your answer sheet.

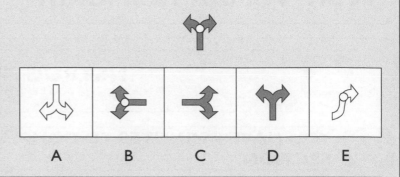

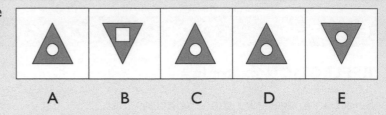

A   B   C   D   E

LEAST SIMILAR Example 3

Select the image that is least similar to the other images.

The correct answer is B. This has already been marked in Example 3 in the Non-Verbal Reasoning section of your answer sheet.

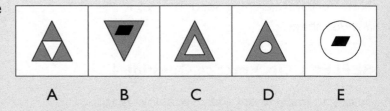

A   B   C   D   E

LEAST SIMILAR Practice Question 3

Select the image that is least similar to the other images.

The correct answer is E. Please mark this in Practice Question 3 in the Non-Verbal Reasoning section of your answer sheet.

A   B   C   D   E

STOP AND WAIT FOR FURTHER INSTRUCTIONS

① Look at the following image. Select the image in the row below that is a rotation of the image.

 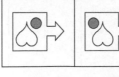

A   B   C   D   E

CONTINUE WORKING

(2) Look at the following image. Select the image in the row below that is a rotation of the image.

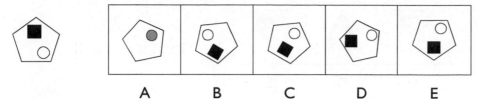

    A   B   C   D   E

(3) Select the image that is least similar to the other images in the row.

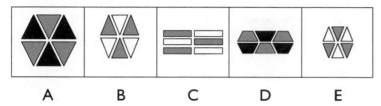

  A   B   C   D   E

(4) Select the image that is least similar to the other images in the row.

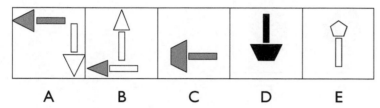

  A   B   C   D   E

(5) Select the image that is least similar to the other images in the row.

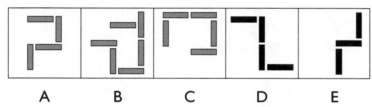

  A   B   C   D   E

(6) Select the image that is least similar to the other images in the row.

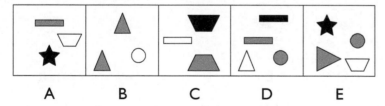

  A   B   C   D   E

(7) Select the image that is least similar to the other images in the row.

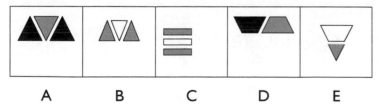

  A   B   C   D   E

CONTINUE WORKING ➡

(8) Select the image that is least similar to the other images in the row.

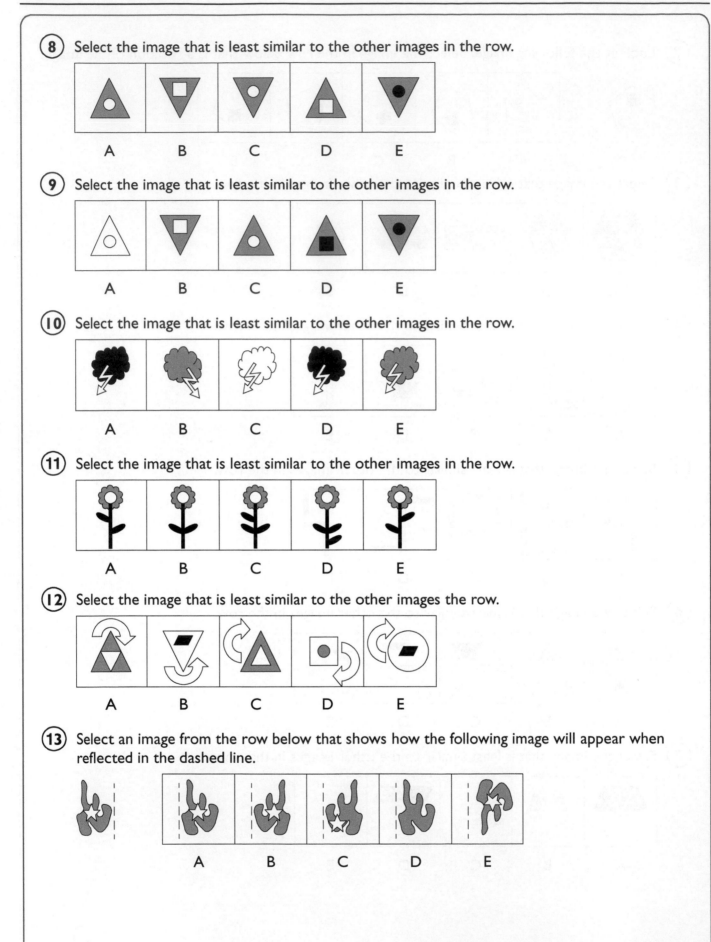

A   B   C   D   E

(9) Select the image that is least similar to the other images in the row.

A   B   C   D   E

(10) Select the image that is least similar to the other images in the row.

A   B   C   D   E

(11) Select the image that is least similar to the other images in the row.

A   B   C   D   E

(12) Select the image that is least similar to the other images the row.

A   B   C   D   E

(13) Select an image from the row below that shows how the following image will appear when reflected in the dashed line.

A   B   C   D   E

CONTINUE WORKING

14 Select an image from the row below that shows how the following image will appear when reflected in the dashed line.

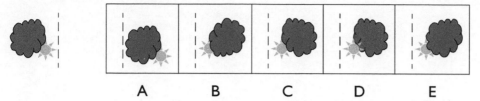

  A   B   C   D   E

15 Select an image from the row below that shows how the following image will appear when reflected in the dashed line.

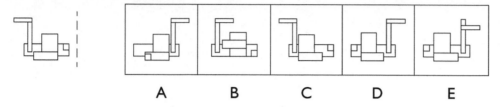

  A   B   C   D   E

END OF PAPER

Test D Paper 2

Instructions

1. Ensure you have pencils and an eraser with you.

2. Make sure you are able to see a clock or watch.

3. Write your name on the answer sheet.

4. Do not open the question booklet until you are told to do so by the audio instructions.

5. Listen carefully to the audio instructions given.

6. Mark your answers on the answer sheet only.

7. All workings must be completed on a separate piece of paper.

8. You should not use a calculator, dictionary or thesaurus at any point in this paper.

9. Move through the papers as quickly as possible and with care.

10. Follow the instructions at the foot of each page.

11. You should mark your answers with a horizontal strike, as shown on the answer sheet.

12. If you want to change your answer, ensure that you rub out your first answer and that your second answer is clearly more visible.

13. You can go back and review any questions that are within the section you are working on only. You must await further instructions before moving onto another section.

Symbols and Phrases used in the Tests

 Instructions  Time allowed for this section Stop and wait for further instructions  Continue working

Cloze Sentences

INSTRUCTIONS

 YOU HAVE 7 MINUTES TO COMPLETE THE FOLLOWING SECTION.

YOU HAVE 17 QUESTIONS TO COMPLETE WITHIN THE TIME GIVEN.

EXAMPLES

A	B	C	D	E	F	G	H	I	J
dog	small	tiny	huge	minute	free	big	enormous	gigantic	penguin

Example 1

Complete the sentence in the most sensible way by selecting an appropriate word from the table above.

The _____ sat by the fire.

The correct answer is A. This has already been marked in Example 1 in the Cloze Sentences section of your answer sheet.

Practice Question 1

Complete the sentence in the most sensible way by selecting an appropriate word from the table above.

The _____ laid an egg.

The correct answer is J. Please mark the answer J in Practice Question 1 in the Cloze Sentences section of your answer sheet.

Example 2

One word in the following sentence has had three letters removed from it. Keeping the letters in the same order, identify the three-letter word that is made from the missing letters.

The pupil could not pay attion.

The correct answer is 'ten'. This has been marked in Example 2 in the Cloze Sentences section of your answer sheet.

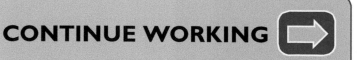

CONTINUE WORKING

Practice Question 2

One word in the following sentence has had three letters removed from it. Keeping the letters in the same order, identify the three-letter word that is made from the missing letters.

She treasu her mother's bracelet.

The correct answer is 'red'. Please mark this in Practice Question 2 in the Cloze Sentences section of your answer sheet.

STOP AND WAIT FOR FURTHER INSTRUCTIONS

Complete the most sensible sentence by selecting an appropriate word from the table below.

A fantastical	B dehydrated	C laborious	D fractured	E subterranean
F extracted	G ruling	H standard	I ample	J adventure

(1) The blood was _____ from the ancient specimen.

(2) The judge's _____ was final.

(3) The _____ cave was dark and cold.

(4) The parking signs gave the residents _____ warning that the road would close at midnight.

(5) The work was painstaking and _____.

(6) The animal's limb was _____ in several places.

(7) The journey came to an end and the _____ was over.

CONTINUE WORKING

(8) The film was a _____ story, set in space.

(9) The athlete's dedication to her training had set a high _____.

(10) After a day of walking in the mountains, the boy felt _____.

One word in the following sentence has had three letters removed from it. Keeping the letters in the same order, identify the three-letter word that is made from the three missing letters.

(11) The hairdresser tmed the girl's hair.

(12) The landse was rugged.

(13) The project failed for one rea.

(14) The boy hed in the glorious sunshine.

(15) The girl's clothes were sped when she splashed in the mud.

(16) Does this car have a sp tyre?

(17) The se of the book had broken and all the pages had fallen out.

STOP AND WAIT FOR FURTHER INSTRUCTIONS ⊗

Problem Solving

INSTRUCTIONS

 YOU HAVE 12 MINUTES TO COMPLETE THE FOLLOWING SECTION.

YOU HAVE 10 QUESTIONS TO COMPLETE WITHIN THE TIME GIVEN.

EXAMPLES

A £2.60	B £3.40	C £2.40	D 25	E £1.35
F £3.40	G 14	H 31	I 28	J 34

Example 1

Calculate the following:

If I buy five apples at 20p each, and four bananas at 35p each, how much change will I receive if I pay with a £5 note.

The correct answer is A. This has already been marked in Example 1 in the Problem Solving section of your answer sheet.

Practice Question 1

Calculate the following:

There are 17 people on a bus when it arrives at a bus stop. Eleven people get on the bus, and three get off. How many people are then left on the bus?

The correct answer is D. Please mark this in Practice Question 1 in the Problem Solving section of your answer sheet.

STOP AND WAIT FOR FURTHER INSTRUCTIONS

Several questions will follow for you to answer.

A 35	B £104	C 8	D 10	E 95
F 7	G 85	H £84	I £94	J 4

Select an answer to each question from the 10 different possible answers in the table above.
You may use an answer for more than one question.

(1) Edward is planning a birthday party at the local zoo. He invites eight boys and four girls. If $\frac{3}{4}$ of the children invited attend the party, and there are two girls at the party, how many boys are at the party (including Edward himself)?

(2) How many children are at the party in total?

(3) At the entrance to the zoo, the following entry prices are displayed:
   Adults £12 each
   Children £8 each
   For groups of 11 or more, £7 (per adult or child)
   If two adults also go to the zoo to supervise the children, what is the total entry cost for the party?

(4) Edward receives some gifts and money from his friends and family for his birthday. He receives a £10 note from each of four friends, £20 from one family member, and a £5 note from each of six other people. Finally, he receives a birthday card with four £1 coins taped inside. How much money did Edward receive for his birthday?

(5) At lunchtime, there is a birthday party lunch at the zoo for everyone in the party group. The zoo provides a set party lunch for each of the adults and children. The cost is £8.50 per child and £9.50 per adult. What is the total cost of the party lunch?

(6) Everyone sits down for lunch at 13:05 and the lunch finishes at 14:40. How long did the lunch last in minutes?

(7) Following lunch, the group decide to go on the zoo train that carries visitors around the zoo. The train stops at various places around the zoo. When the entire party boarded the train, there were already 68 people on board. At the next stop, 13 other zoo visitors alight from the train, and a further 18 visitors board the train. How many people are on the train at that point?

CONTINUE WORKING

8 The next stop for the train is the tiger and lion enclosures, which are very popular. 78 of the passengers alight from the train at this point. Nobody is able to board the train at this stop. How many people are on the train after the 78 people have alighted?

9 The party get off the train at the final destination which is the aquarium. The time at this point is 15:25. How many minutes were they on board the train if they first boarded the train at 14:50?

10 The group left the aquarium quite late in the day. The train had stopped running for the day at this point. The group had only 15 minutes to reach the exit of the zoo before it was locked at 5 p.m. If the zoo exit was 1 km from the aquarium, at what speed in km/h did they have to walk in order to reach the exit at closing time, at the latest?

STOP AND WAIT FOR FURTHER INSTRUCTIONS

Antonyms

INSTRUCTIONS

 YOU HAVE 10 MINUTES TO COMPLETE THE FOLLOWING SECTION.

YOU HAVE 25 QUESTIONS TO COMPLETE WITHIN THE TIME GIVEN.

Examples

Example 1

Select the word that is least similar to the following word:

light

A	B	C	D	E
dark	water	feather	bright	hill

The correct answer is A. This has already been marked in Example 1 in the Antonyms section of your answer sheet.

Practice Question 1

Select the word that is least similar to the following word:

smooth

A	B	C	D	E
allow	beneath	rough	whilst	shade

The correct answer is C. Please mark the answer C in Practice Question 1 in the Antonyms section of your answer sheet.

STOP AND WAIT FOR FURTHER INSTRUCTIONS

In each row, select the word from the table that is least similar to the word above the table.

(1) educated

A	B	C	D	E
familiar	uninformed	mourning	forgiveness	unusual

(2) implausible

A	B	C	D	E
nimble	vulgar	frenetic	logical	impossible

(3) pensioner

A	B	C	D	E
proficient	impressionable	draft	infant	inept

(4) bald

A	B	C	D	E
sulk	restriction	flair	custom	hairy

(5) customer

A	B	C	D	E
modest	tradesman	sense	retreat	direct

(6) neglect

A	B	C	D	E
nourish	congeal	outgoing	urgency	refinement

CONTINUE WORKING ⇨

(7) glistening

A	B	C	D	E
dull	friendship	gleaming	timely	tangle

(8) casual

A	B	C	D	E
digress	slovenly	interior	planned	result

(9) occupy

A	B	C	D	E
fickle	vacate	agitated	resort	retrieve

(10) invigorated

A	B	C	D	E
receptacle	jovial	tired	slender	vivid

(11) compress

A	B	C	D	E
superlative	restrain	mirth	determine	expand

(12) debt

A	B	C	D	E
profit	fad	fiscal	verdict	spectre

CONTINUE WORKING ⇨

13 glamorous

A	B	C	D	E
immaterial	plain	commode	majestic	attractive

14 auxiliary

A	B	C	D	E
prudent	harrowing	main	apprehend	gaunt

15 uneven

A	B	C	D	E
detested	predictive	merriment	level	revelation

16 truth

A	B	C	D	E
beg	rumour	parameter	unkempt	gumption

17 concentrate

A	B	C	D	E
earnest	profanity	dilute	solitude	tendency

18 subdue

A	B	C	D	E
aggravate	forecast	typical	quell	subtlety

CONTINUE WORKING ➡

19 minute

A	B	C	D	E
estimate	inhibit	timely	colossal	immature

20 demolish

A	B	C	D	E
rotund	destruct	resent	undulation	assemble

21 stable

A	B	C	D	E
equilibrium	imbalanced	jovial	reveal	august

22 love

A	B	C	D	E
fondness	beloved	enamoured	animosity	devotion

23 finale

A	B	C	D	E
elitist	opening	jaunt	conclusion	supreme

24 leader

A	B	C	D	E
tireless	consume	follower	guide	shaded

25 mundane

A	B	C	D	E
recapitulate	severe	drowsy	exciting	innate

STOP AND WAIT FOR FURTHER INSTRUCTIONS ⊗

Non-Verbal Reasoning

 YOU HAVE 8 MINUTES TO COMPLETE THE FOLLOWING SECTION.

YOU HAVE 15 QUESTIONS TO COMPLETE WITHIN THE TIME GIVEN.

EXAMPLES

CUBES Example 1

Look at the cube net.

Select the only cube that could be formed from the net above.

The correct answer is E. This has already been marked in Example 1 in the Non-Verbal Reasoning section of your answer sheet.

A   B   C   D   E

CUBES Practice Question 1

Look at the cube net.

Select the only cube that could be formed from the net above.

The correct answer is A. Please mark this in Practice Question 1 in the Non-Verbal Reasoning section of your answer sheet.

A   B   C   D   E

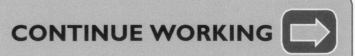 **CONTINUE WORKING**

REFLECTION Example 2

Select an image from the row below that shows how the following shape or pattern will appear when reflected.

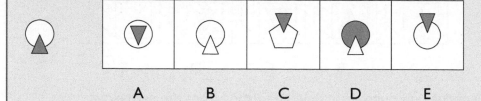

A   B   C   D   E

The correct answer is E. This has already been marked in Example 2 in the Non-Verbal Reasoning section of your answer sheet.

REFLECTION Practice Question 2

Select an image from the row below that shows how the following shape or pattern will appear when reflected.

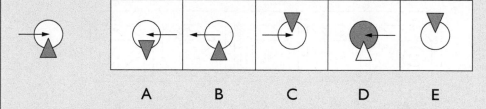

A   B   C   D   E

The correct answer is C. Please mark this in Practice Question 2 in the Non-Verbal Reasoning section of your answer sheet.

STOP AND WAIT FOR FURTHER INSTRUCTIONS

(1) Look at the cube net. Select the only cube that could be formed from the net below.

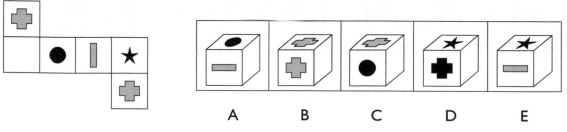

A   B   C   D   E

CONTINUE WORKING

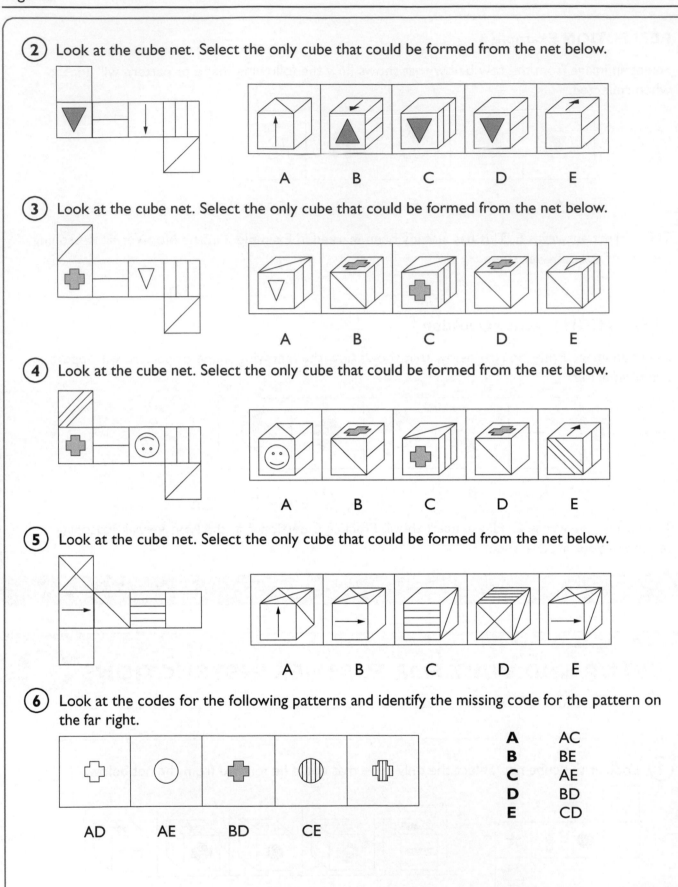

② Look at the cube net. Select the only cube that could be formed from the net below.

A   B   C   D   E

③ Look at the cube net. Select the only cube that could be formed from the net below.

A   B   C   D   E

④ Look at the cube net. Select the only cube that could be formed from the net below.

A   B   C   D   E

⑤ Look at the cube net. Select the only cube that could be formed from the net below.

A   B   C   D   E

⑥ Look at the codes for the following patterns and identify the missing code for the pattern on the far right.

AD   AE   BD   CE

A	AC
B	BE
C	AE
D	BD
E	CD

CONTINUE WORKING

(7) Look at the codes for the following patterns and identify the missing code for the pattern on the far right.

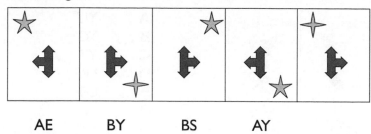

AE   BY   BS   AY

A   BS
B   AS
C   BE
D   AE
E   BY

(8) Look at the codes for the following patterns and identify the missing code for the pattern on the far right.

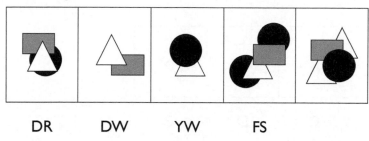

DR   DW   YW   FS

A   YS
B   FS
C   DS
D   DY
E   YR

(9) Look at the codes for the following patterns and identify the missing code for the pattern on the far right.

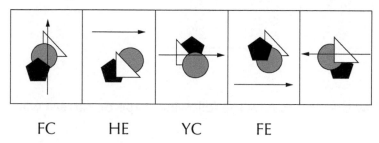

FC   HE   YC   FE

A   HE
B   YC
C   HC
D   FE
E   FY

(10) Look at the codes for the following patterns and identify the missing code for the pattern on the far right.

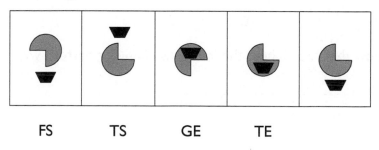

FS   TS   GE   TE

A   TS
B   GE
C   GS
D   FE
E   FS

CONTINUE WORKING ⟶

(11) Look at the codes for the following patterns and identify the missing code for the pattern on the far right.

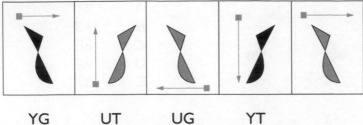

YG   UT   UG   YT

A   YU
B   YG
C   YT
D   UG
E   UT

(12) Select an image from the row below that shows how the following shape or pattern will appear when reflected.

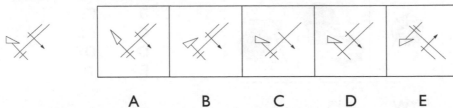

A   B   C   D   E

(13) Select an image from the row below that shows how the following shape or pattern will appear when reflected.

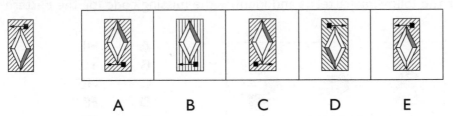

A   B   C   D   E

(14) Select an image from the row below that shows how the following shape or pattern will appear when reflected.

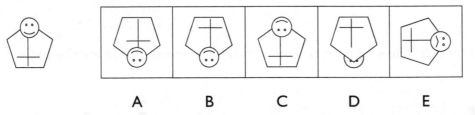

A   B   C   D   E

(15) Select an image from the row below that shows how the following shape or pattern will appear when reflected.

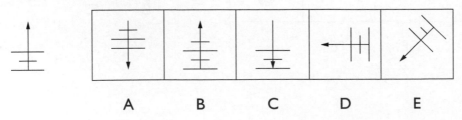

A   B   C   D   E

Shuffled Sentences

INSTRUCTIONS

 YOU HAVE 8 MINUTES TO COMPLETE THE FOLLOWING SECTION.

YOU HAVE 15 QUESTIONS TO COMPLETE WITHIN THE TIME GIVEN.

EXAMPLES

Example 1

The following sentence is shuffled and also contains one unnecessary word. Rearrange the sentence correctly, in order to identify the unnecessary word.

dog the ran fetch the to stick gluing.

A	B	C	D	E
gluing	dog	ran	the	stick

The correct answer is A. This has already been marked in Example 1 in the Shuffled Sentences section of your answer sheet.

Practice Question 1

The following sentence is shuffled and also contains one unnecessary word. Rearrange the sentence correctly, in order to identify the unnecessary word.

pushed Emma stood up and closed the table under the chairs.

A	B	C	D	E
chairs	stood	under	closed	Emma

The correct answer is D. Please mark this in Practice Question 1 in the Shuffled Sentences section of your answer sheet.

STOP AND WAIT FOR FURTHER INSTRUCTIONS

Each of the following sentences is shuffled and also contains one unnecessary word.
Rearrange the sentence correctly, in order to identify the unnecessary word.

(1) beautiful sea shelled house overlooking live we but the small a in.

A	B	C	D	E
shelled	a	house	overlooking	the

(2) chimney misty moonlit the stars in twinkled the sky was and air the.

A	B	C	D	E
and	chimney	misty	was	the

(3) unbeatable shop noisy overpriced discounts was advert the stated but the.

A	B	C	D	E
but	was	the	stated	noisy

(4) entrance van site candidly the the of the at parked was.

A	B	C	D	E
the	site	candidly	was	van

(5) hand by mine ancient dug digger was the subterranean

A	B	C	D	E
digger	dug	the	by	hand

(6) sunrise sight stirred emotions tears the of my the.

A	B	C	D	E
the	tears	of	my	sight

(7) in test marks tables achieved boy the full achievement times his.

A	B	C	D	E
to	achieved	achievement	went	tables

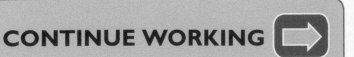

CONTINUE WORKING

8 stabilised enforced steel tunnel the with was.

A	B	C	D	E
the	was	tunnel	enforced	with

9 unemployment many problem countries in is a high there.

A	B	C	D	E
there	countries	in	problem	a

10 shone the dazzling sunlight in the packet diamond.

A	B	C	D	E
diamond	shone	in	the	packet

11 bag landed collected he school son as missing was his noticed he that from his.

A	B	C	D	E
his	was	landed	that	from

12 talking questions the the carefully listen have you elongated answer to people to to.

A	B	C	D	E
talking	to	you	the	elongated

13 rounded bag evidence a in the placed he.

A	B	C	D	E
in	placed	a	rounded	he

14 up for let's view hill go the run a.

A	B	C	D	E
let's	view	a	the	for

CONTINUE WORKING

15 looked looking plant strange at this look.

A	B	C	D	E
look	at	this	looking	looked

looked looking plant strange at this look.

END OF PAPER

Answers to Test C Paper 1

Comprehension

1 C
Verb
2 A
Allotments are very popular
3 E
Allotments require people to spend time and effort.
4 D
Nothing happens
5 B
A busy place
6 A
A large quantity
7 D
Envelop
8 E
Every seven days
9 D
Repel
10 B
Noun

Grammar

1 E
No errors
2 C
she
3 C
got
4 D
is wore out,"
5 E
No errors
6 C
she hurted her leg
7 C
emily realised
8 A
"Lets run
9 D
no further

Numeracy

Q1 E
14, as 7 (a third of 21) is half the number

Q2 C
37, +1 +2 +3 +4 are the differences between consecutive numbers in the sequence

Q3 A
4,1,1,1 as 4 − 1 = 3 in the units column, then in the tens column, the original number must have been 1 which when 1 hundred is borrowed and converted into tens makes the original 1 into 11, and 11 − 8 = 3. The 9 in the hundreds column has now become an 8, so 8 − 7 = 1, and 4 − 0 = 4 in the thousands column.

Q4 E
12 minutes, 8 miles per hour (or 60 minutes) means 1.6 miles will be travelled in 1.6 ÷ 8 × 60 = 12 minutes.

Q5 D
£6, as £24 is the price paid after the discount i.e. 80% of the original price. So 20% must be £24 ÷ 4 = £6.

Q6 B
11, Emily and William are twins, so are the same age (7). Mohammed is 4 years older, 7 + 4 = 11 years old.

Q7 A
$\frac{1}{10}$ m, 101 mm, 10.11 cm, 11 cm, 10 km, as there are 100 cm in 1 m and 1,000 mm in 1 m. Converting all options to cm gives: 10 cm, 10.1 cm, 10.11 cm, 11 cm, 1,000,000 cm

Q8 A
453 − 2 = 452 − 0, as 451 is not the same as 452, and the other answer options are all equal on left and right sides of the equation.

Q9 E
676, as 26 × 20 = 520, and 6 × 26 = 156, 520 + 156 = 676

Q10 D
8.75 midway between 8.5 and 9

Q11 B
1 : 20 p.m. (add 4 hours to get 1 : 25 pm, and then deduct 5 minutes)

Q12 C
$\frac{1}{9}$, as to make the fraction 3 times smaller requires multiplying the denominator by 3.

Q13 **A**

15, 23 + 7 = 30 and half of 30 is 15

Q14 **E**

2,500 m, converted to cm in real life the churches are 0.5 × 500,000 = 250,000 cm apart = 2,500 m (by dividing by 100)

Q15 **D**

520 as there are 1,000 g in 1 kg, so it is necessary to multiply by 1,000.

Q16 **A**

0.77, 1% of 70 is $\frac{1}{100}$ of 70 = 0.7. So 1.1% of 70 is 1.1 times 0.7, or 0.7 + 0.07 = 0.77

Q17 **A**

5, as 5 × 15 = 75

Q18 **D**

basketball, identified by the smallest segment of the chart with the lowest number of children choosing this hobby.

Q19 **A**

3 as the mode is the most frequently occurring piece of data.

Q20 **B**

Australia, which has the second highest number of medals after the UK.

Q21 **A**

3.5, arranging the 10 pieces of data in order of size gives 1,2,3,3,3,4,5,5,7,8 and the median is the middle of this data (in this case the middle of 2 numbers as there is an even number of pieces of data). Halfway between the 5th and 6th pieces of data is 3.5.

Q22 **D**

4.1 as the sum of all of the data is 41. The mean is calculated by dividing this by the number of pieces of data, which gives an answer of 4.1.

Q23 **B**

3 as this is the overlapping section of the data sets.

Q24 **C**

25, i.e. 8 + 5 + 11 + 1 = 25 which is the sum of all numbers outside of the Peugeot set.

Q25 **A**

12, which is 8 + 4, this is represented by the area within the Porsche set but excluding any numbers that may be within the Audi set (so exclude the 5 + 2).

Q26 **D**

2 because they are represented by the overlapping part of all 3 sets.

Q27 **A**

1 represented by the overlapping Audi and Peugeot set which is not within the Porsche set (so need to exclude the 2).

Q28 **E**

3, 9, 3, 5, 5

The sum of the bottom row is 15, so all rows columns and diagonals sum to 15 (as noted in the question). Next calculate c is 3, then e is 5, so d is 5. Then a must be 3, and finally b is 9.

Q29 **B**

100, $99 - \frac{p}{10} = 89$, so $\frac{p}{10}$ must be 10, and so p must be 100.

Q30 **D**

65, dividing the marbles up in the ratio 5:1:1 gives both Julia and Mark 91 divided by 7 (5 + 1 + 1) = 13 marbles each. Mike has 91 ÷ 7 × 5 = 65 marbles.

Q31 **C**

10, as the perimeter is 10b + 1 = 101, so 10b = 100, and b is therefore 10.

Q32 **A**

113.333 (make question easier by multiplying both numbers by 100 to eliminate the decimal point to give 1,700 divided by 15)

Q33 **A**

men 6, women 8, children 29

Women = 43 − 35 = 8, and this means of the 14 adults, 6 must be men, which in turn means that 29 of the 35 men and children are actually children.

Q34 **C**

51 (1 + 5 + 31 + 14 = 51) The 1 must be added in as the dates are inclusive in the question.

Q35 **E**

20.14 as 16.29 add 3 hours and 45 minutes gives 20.14 (could add on 4 hours then subtract 15 minutes).

Q36 **E**

40°

The left triangle is isosceles in which 2 of the angles are 50°, and the other angle is 80°

which is at the bottom right of the triangle. Using the fact that all of the interior angles in the quadrilateral (4 sided shape) sum to 360°, the missing angle is calculated as 360° − 130° − 50° − 50° − 90° = 40°

Q37 C

65°

Angle d is 180° − 100° − 60° = 20°.
So angle c is 70°. So angle e must be 180° − 70° − 45° = 65°

Q38 D

1100

Can work out either the Euro to Pounds exchange rate of 660 ÷ 600 = 1.1 or Dollar to Pound exchange rate of 900 ÷ 600 = 1.5 from the data given in the table.
Use either of these to calculate the number of pounds. 1,210 ÷ 1.1 = 1,100 or 1,650 ÷ 1.5 = 1,100

Q39 A

length 48 cm, width 4 cm

Write length (l) in terms of width (w) to establish perimeter in terms of width,
Perimeter = w + 12w + w + 12w = 26w
Perimeter from question is 104 cm
So 26w = 104
w = 4, so l = 48 (12 × 4)
Alternatively the same method could be followed by writing the width in terms of length, but this may be more challenging.

Synonyms

Q1	E	guarantee	Q11 D supple	
Q2	D	courteous	Q12 A wring	
Q3	A	frenzied	Q13 B neutral	
Q4	D	thrive	Q14 A eavesdrop	
Q5	A	border	Q15 C comprehend	
Q6	E	nimbleness	Q16 A clothing	
Q7	C	unruly	Q17 B oppose	
Q8	A	artificial	Q18 E foe	
Q9	A	imperial	Q19 A deceitful	
Q10	D	masquerade	Q20 D unravel	

Non-Verbal Reasoning

Q1 D

Alternating circle size, increasing count on horizontal lines, background is diagonal line, foreground circle.

Q2 C

Alternating circle size, increasing count on horizontal lines, small circle should be in the background, with diagonal line in the foreground.

Q3 D

Outer line of five black squares are moving around the outside of the overall grid in an anti-clockwise direction, grey squares moving diagonally towards top left, and striped square always follows grey.

Q4 B

Five triangles and the star are moving anti-clockwise around the overall grid. Alternating outer and inner are solid black triangles and striped triangles. Within triangles are star and grey triangle, again alternating position.

Q5 D

The arrows switch between pointing left and right, as well as alternating between being in the background and foreground in relation to the triangle.

Q6 B

Each row has one grey and one white arrow. These are combined in the other square on each row, with the white always in the foreground and grey in the background. Diagonal from bottom left to top right is sum of other 2 in row, with white in the foreground.

Q7 B

Each column has one of each of the three images featured in the overall grid. The black square is the missing square in the middle column.

Q8 B

Others are reflections or do not include all of the image.

Q9 D

A is a reflection of the image on the left. Must ensure that the dot remains in the same relative position to the arrow when the overall image is rotated.

Answers to Test C Paper 2

Cloze Sentences

Q1 D
dentist, teeth
The dentist took time to reassure me before starting work on my teeth.

Q2 C
Despite, time, guests
Despite the shortfall in numbers, a good time was had by all guests.

Q3 B
weather, recently
They were hoping the weather would be better than it had been recently.

Q4 C
support, nation
The support of the nation was behind the athletes.

Q5 D
depth, sympathy
The depth of sympathy was very much appreciated by the mourners.

Q6 C
ambulance, scene
The ambulance rushed to the scene.

Q7 D
Who, guess
Who would arrive first was anybody's guess.

Q8 C
outcome, imminently
The outcome of the court case was due imminently.

Q9 D
monkey, smiled, camera
The monkey perched on her shoulder and smiled for the camera.

Q10 C
magician, never
How the magician managed to do that, I will never know!

Q11 tin
The flowers were attracting the butterflies.

Q12 lit
The instability of the suspension bridge meant closure was the only option.

Q13 hot
The photocopier had run out of paper.

Q14 den
They were feeling confident as they set out on their expedition.

Q15 pad
They enjoyed paddling their feet in the sea on the hot summer's day.

Q16 low
They decided to meet up the following month.

Q17 Eve
Every little detail had been considered.

Problem Solving

Q1 I
27
There are $15 \div 5 \times 4$ girls = 12 girls and 15 boys = 27 children in the class.

Q2 H
10
Sam is 6 in two years' time, so Sarah will then be 12. Now (two years earlier), Sarah is 10.

Q3 A
53
$76 - 23 = 53$ children.

Q4 D
£52
$27 - 1 = 26$ children (excluding Sarah);
$6 \times £5 + 2 \times £2 + (26 - 8) \times £1 = £52$

Q5 G
9
Floor area = $8 \times 4 = 32$ square metres. 4 tiles (2×2) will fit exactly into each square metre. So $4 \times 32 = 128$ tiles are required to cover the floor. $128 \div 15 = 8$ remainder 8, so 9 boxes will be required.

Q6 F
5
60 divided by 12

Q7 E
£41.40
$23 \times 1.80 = £41.40$

Q8 J
£35
Each tube costs $20 \times 3.5 = 70p$, so 50 tubes cost £35

Q9 B

12

Girls = 174 − 99 = 75, so teachers
= 87 − 75 = 12

Q10 C

£527

Money raised = 123 × £5 = £615 from the
books of tickets. Individual tickets raised a
further 60 × 20p = £12. Total is £615 + £12
= £627. £100 special prize is deducted from
the £627 to leave £527.

Antonyms

Q1 B *stale*

Q2 D *mobile*

Q3 E *gradual*

Q4 A *crooked*

Q5 D *inferior*

Q6 C *wild*

Q7 D *enormous*

Q8 A *separate*

Q9 D *occupied*

Q10 E *vague*

Q11 E *worse*

Q12 B *separate*

Q13 D *discourage*

Q14 E *export*

Q15 A *fade*

Q16 A *limited*

Q17 C *increase*

Q18 E *deny*

Q19 C *inaction*

Q20 A *clear*

Q21 C *constant*

Q22 E *displeasure*

Q23 E *disorder*

Q24 B *professional*

Q25 A *foreign*

Non-Verbal Reasoning

Q1 A

BY

First letter relates to whether arrows cross or
not, second letter relates to the appearance
of the non curved arrow(s).

Q2 D

RS

First letter relates to number of shapes,
second letter relates to the number of
triangles.

Q3 E

YA

First letter relates to shape at the bottom,
second letter relates to the shape at the top.

Q4 B

YA

First letter relates to number of double
ended arrows, second letter relates to
orientation of the square shape with the
arrows coming from it.

Q5 A

Connection is outer arrow is rotated a
quarter turn anti-clockwise. Also inner arrow
is rotated clockwise.

Q6 A

Large shape turns upside down, dark arrow
switches from the right hand side of the large
shape to left hand side. Light arrow changes
from the top to the bottom, also changes
direction from pointing left to pointing right
and changes the arrow base from a square
to circle.

Q7 C

Outer shape is inverted (reflected in a
horizontal line), inner grey shape transforms
into a large grey square.

Q8 A

The outer shape is inverted, the middle
square has become black and smaller. The
cross disappears.

Q9 D

The triangle alternates from top left to
bottom right corners, the horizontal arrow
moves up the diagonal from bottom left to
top right. The other arrows remain vertical.

Q10 C

The arrows rotate anti-clockwise around
the perimeter of the square. The number
of circles increases and the inner hexagon
appears in alternate squares as the sequence
progresses.

Q11 C

The triangle moves through the sequence
of three shapes, from back to front as the
sequence progresses. The triangle will be in
the middle of the three shapes in the blank
grid. The three shapes are moving around
the perimeter of the grid in an anti-clockwise
direction.

Q12 A

The arrow moves down the grids as the
sequence progresses, alternating between the
middle two columns. The pairs of black and
grey dots move down and up the grids.

Q13 D

The number of sides on the shapes increase in an anti-clockwise direction around the corners of the grid. The sides increase from 3 to 4, to 5 therefore the shape in the top right should have six sides. The shapes in the corners of the diagonals are the same colour, ie the hexagon should be grey.

Q14 B

The bottom row and middle row are combined in the top row, with the bottom row being in the foreground and the middle row being in the background.

Q15 E

The top and bottom rows combine to make the middle row with the top row in the foreground and bottom row in the background.

Shuffled Sentences

Q1 A

an

Debris was strewn across the neighbourhood's streets as a result of last night's storm.

Q2 A

whether

The bad weather caused severe delays to flights at the airport.

Q3 D

those

This is likely to make a big difference.

Q4 A

tree

She decided to leaf through the book whilst in the bookshop

Q5 D

although

It was now the responsibility of the parents.

Q6 B

there

The scores were all checked to confirm their accuracy.

Q7 C

scene

She was astounded by what she had just seen.

Q8 D

mirrored

The central location was ideal for them.

Q9 A

hanging

The basket was positioned in the hallway.

Q10 B

sunk

Several attempts were made to recover the cargo.

Q11 D

taken

The journey took three hours by car.

Q12 A

kicked

The dress code stipulated formal attire for the annual charity ball.

Q13 A

waist

The chest of drawers provided extra storage in the bedroom.

Q14 D

must

Use of cameras was prohibited in the theatre.

Q15 B

accept

A discount was offered in return for payment in cash.

Answers to Test D Paper 1

Comprehension

1. **C**

Body language and eye movements

2. **E**

To further their career and to bring them success

3. **C**

Misunderstood

4. **D**

The details from the meetings can be easily sent to a significant amount of people.

5. B

The size of mobile phones has reduced and their capabilities have increased.

6. A

A large number of emails are unread or deleted.

7. B

Adjective

8. C

An item that people use in their everyday life

9. A

User-friendly

10. C

Elderly people are being taught how to communicate via social media.

Numeracy

1. D

3004

2. B

23

$144 - 121 = 23$

3. E

98

$294 \div 3 = 98$

4. D

108°

interior + exterior $= 180°$

exterior $= 360 \div 5$ (number of sides) $= 72°$

interior $= 180 - 72 = 108°$

5. C

4

Substitute information in the question:

$4 = 2a - 4$

so rearranged,

$8 = 2a$, and $a = 4$

6. D

1

Substitute information in the question:

$8a - 8 = 0$, so $8a = 8$, and $a = 1$

7. B

5

$15 + ? = 20$, so $? = 5$

8. B

10

$8 \times ? = 72 + 8$

$8 \times ? = 80$

$? = 10$

9. E

15

$? + 15 = 30$

$? = 15$

10. C

2

1 roll costs £1.50 × 3 = £4.50

For £10, I can buy 2 rolls costing £9 and I will have £1 left over.

11. E

1 in 6

The number the die lands on does not depend on the previous throws, and there are 6 faces which are equally likely for the die to land on.

12. A

16

$5 + 22 - 11 = 16$

13. B

5

15 would like pizza. Of the 15 pizza slices, one-third were not eaten, so 5 remain.

14. C

35

From right to left, the sequence increases by an increasing amount, with each difference being 1 higher than the last. Differences are 2, 3, 4, 5 so next is a difference of 6 (added onto 29 to give 35).

15. C

26

16. B

8

56 divided by 7 = 8

17. D

96

Headlines are shown 4 times per hour,

4×24 (hours in a day) $= 96$

18. A

1.6

Difference is doubling between each consecutive pair of numbers in the sequence. Next difference is 0.8.

19. B

one-fifth of 160

In order of answers: 31, 32, 31.5, 31, 31.33

20. E

9

$5 - 3 + 7 = 9$

21. D

57

Range is highest less the lowest $= 81 - 24 = 57$

22. A

52.5

Mean is the sum of the data, divided by the number of pieces of data = 420 ÷ 8 = 52.5

23. C

58.5

Find middle data value when arranged in size order:

24, 24, 34, 53, 64, 68, 72, 81 so halfway between 53 and 64, which is 117 ÷ 2 = 58.5

24. C

40

25. A

2006–2012

Need to find the only 2 years listed in the answers between which the % of the higher value is 5 times that of the lower.

26. E

2012–2013

27. C

32 and $\frac{1}{3}$

Divide the sum of the data by 9 (the number of pieces of data).

291 ÷ 9 = 32.333

28. D

89

One additional year means there are now 10 years. This means that as the mean is 38, the total of all 10 years data must be 10 x 38 = 380. After 9 years, the sum was 291, so the 10th year (2014) must be 380 − 291 = 89% of children.

Synonyms

1. **B** routinely
2. **D** distort
3. **A** vitality
4. **E** unfold
5. **B** remember
6. **B** company
7. **C** classic
8. **E** admission
9. **B** spirited
10. **D** gratitude
11. **A** hurry
12. **E** amount
13. **B** devour
14. **E** civilised
15. **E** happy
16. **B** emanate
17. **C** polite
18. **D** tranquil
19. **B** lessen
20. **C** series

Non-Verbal Reasoning

1. **B**

This is a half turn of the original image.

2. **D**

This is a quarter turn anticlockwise of the original image.

3. **C**

The only answer where closing the shapes together does not make a hexagon.

4. **B**

The only answer where the rectangle and the shape it leads into are not the same shade. (There is shading on one of the triangles, but not on the rectangle.)

5. **B**

The only answer where the rectangles do not join at the ends – one joins another rectangle in the middle.

6. **B**

The only answer where there are not black, grey and white shapes.

7. **E**

The only answer where closing the shapes together makes a 3-sided shape, rather than a quadrilateral. E is also the only image made up of different-sized shapes.

8. **E**

The only answer where there is not a white shape inside.

9. **A**

The only answer where there is not a grey triangle in the background.

10. **B**

The only answer where the arrow does not point to the left.

11. **D**

The only answer where the stem is in background, and flower in foreground.

12. **B**

The only answer where the arrow is rotating anticlockwise.

13. **B**
14. **C**
15. **D**

Answers to Test D Paper 2

Cloze Sentences

1. **F**
   The blood was **extracted** from the ancient specimen.
2. **G**
   The judge's **ruling** was final.
3. **E**
   The **subterranean** cave was dark and cold.
4. **I**
   The parking signs gave the residents **ample** warning that the road would close at midnight.
5. **C**
   The work was painstaking and **laborious**.
6. **D**
   The animal's limb was **fractured** in several places.
7. **J**
   The journey came to an end and the **adventure** was over.
8. **A**
   The film was a **fantastical** story, set in space.
9. **H**
   The athlete's dedication to her training had set a high **standard**.
10. **B**
    After a day of walking in the mountains, the boy felt **dehydrated**.
11. **rim**
    The hairdresser **trim**med the girl's hair.
12. **cap**
    The lands**cap**e was rugged.
13. **son**
    The project failed for one rea**son**.
14. **bat**
    The boy **bat**hed in the glorious sunshine.
15. **oil**
    The girl's clothes were sp**oil**ed when she splashed in the mud.
16. **are**
    Does this car have a sp**are** tyre?
17. **pin**
    The s**pin**e of the book had broken and all the pages had fallen out.

Problem Solving

1. **C**
   8
   $\frac{3}{4}$ of 12 = 9, 9 − 2 = 7, plus Edward equals 8
2. **D**
   10
   $\left(\frac{3}{4} \text{ of } 12 + 1\right)$
3. **H**
   £84
   10 + 2 = 12 × 7 = £84
4. **I**
   £94
5. **B**
   £104
   (8.50 × 10) + (9.50 × 2)
6. **E**
   1 hour and 35 minutes = 95 minutes
7. **G**
   85
   68 + 12 − 13 + 18 = 85
8. **F**
   7
   85 from previous question less 78 = 7
9. **A**
   35
10. **J**
    4
    1 km in 15 minutes is the same as walking at 4 km/h as 1 hour is 60 minutes, and in 60 minutes they would cover 4 km.

Antonyms

1. **B** uninformed
2. **D** logical
3. **D** infant
4. **E** hairy
5. **B** tradesman
6. **A** nourish
7. **A** dull
8. **D** planned
9. **B** vacate
10. **C** tired
11. **E** expand
12. **A** profit
13. **B** plain
14. **C** main
15. **D** level
16. **B** rumour
17. **C** dilute
18. **A** aggravate

19. **D** *colossal*
20. **E** *assemble*
21. **B** *imbalanced*
22. **D** *animosity*
23. **B** *opening*
24. **C** *follower*
25. **D** *exciting*

Non-Verbal Reasoning

1. **C**
   Net requires half-turn rotation, use the cross that will then be on top.
2. **D**
   No rotation of net required.
3. **B**
   No rotation of net required.
4. **A**
   Net requires half-turn rotation.
5. **D**
   Net requires half-turn rotation.
6. **E**
   CD The first letter relates to the shading. The second letter relates to the shape.
7. **C**
   BE The first letter relates to the position of the arrows. The second letter relates to the position of the star.
8. **A**
   YS The first letter relates to the shape in the foreground. The second letter relates to the number of shapes.
9. **C**
   HC The first letter relates to the shape in the foreground. The second letter relates to whether the arrow crosses the shapes.
10. **A**
    TS The first letter relates to the position of the $\frac{3}{4}$ circle. The second letter relates to whether the trapezium overlaps the $\frac{3}{4}$ circle.
11. **D**
    UG The first letter relates to the shading of the shape. The second letter relates to the position of the shape. The arrows are irrelevant.
12. **E**
    Reflection in a horizontal line.
13. **D**
    Reflection in a vertical line.
14. **B**
    Reflection in a horizontal line.
15. **D**
    Reflection in a diagonal line to the top right or bottom left of the image.

Shuffled Sentences

1. **A**
   shelled
   We live in a small but beautiful house overlooking the sea.
2. **B**
   chimney
   The stars twinkled in the moonlit sky and the air was misty.
3. **E**
   noisy
   The advert stated unbeatable discounts but the shop was overpriced.
4. **C**
   candidly
   The van was parked at the entrance of the site.
5. **A**
   digger
   The ancient subterranean mine was dug by hand.
6. **B**
   tears
   The sight of the sunrise stirred my emotions.
7. **C**
   achievement
   The boy achieved full marks in his times tables test.
   The words 'to' and 'went' do not appear in the shuffled sentence and can be eliminated immediately.
8. **D**
   enforced
   The tunnel was stabilised with steel.
9. **A**
   there
   High unemployment is a problem in many countries.

10. *E*

packet

The diamond shone in the dazzling sunlight.

11. *C*

landed

As he collected his son from school he noticed that his bag was missing.

12. *E*

elongated

You have to listen carefully to the people talking to answer the questions.

13. *D*

rounded

He placed the evidence in a bag.

14. *B*

view

Let's go for a run up the hill.

15. *E*

looked

Look at this strange looking plant.